The book of
THE DOG

The book of
THE DOG

Paul Hamlyn
London • New York • Sydney • Toronto

CONTENTS

1 THE EVOLUTION AND DOMESTICATION OF THE DOG 5
by Jane Marks

2 DOGS IN MYTHOLOGY 15
by Michael Stapleton

3 FARM DOGS 28
by John Holmes

4 TOY DOGS IN ART 44
by E. G. Russell Roberts

5 RACING DOGS 62
by Wendy Boorer

6 DOGS OF FILM AND TELEVISION 79
by John Holmes

7 HEROIC DOGS 92
by Stephanie Denham

8 THE CARE AND MANAGEMENT OF DOGS 113
by D.T.M. Forrest, B.V.M. & S., M.R.C.V.S.

9 BREEDS OF DOGS 130
by Wendy Boorer

ACKNOWLEDGMENTS 151

Published by
THE HAMLYN PUBLISHING GROUP LIMITED
LONDON · NEW YORK · SYDNEY · TORONTO
Hamlyn House, Feltham, Middlesex, England
© Copyright 1970 The Hamlyn Publishing Group Limited
Printed in Czechoslovakia by Svoboda, Prague
ISBN 0 600 00458 9
T 2152

THE EVOLUTION AND DOMESTICATION OF THE DOG 1

The wild dogs of the world, together with the domestic dogs, are grouped into a single zoological family, called the *Canidae*. One branch includes the domestic dogs, the wolves, jackals and foxes; the other contains the African hunting dog, the Indian wild dog or dhole, and the South American bush dog. They are all carnivores, feeding mainly on the flesh of animals, which they run down, rather than stalk or ambush. Their hunting is made the more successful by the fact that they are social animals, working together in family groups, or sometimes larger packs. The young are educated in hunting techniques, and the aged and infirm are sometimes cared for. The foxes are the exception, in that outside the breeding and cub rearing season they live in pairs, or may even be solitary. All of the dogs are long distance runners, with excellent powers of scenting and following up their prey, but the factor which was probably of the greatest importance in domestication, was their high level of intelligence. This enables dogs to behave in a more flexible manner than almost any other animal; an attribute which has frequently made the dog a partner, rather than merely a servant of man.

Ancestral dogs are known from fossils, most of them dating back less than 40 million years. They show us how dogs have developed from small, tree-climbing creatures, to fast-running, open country animals. The forerunner of all of the dog family is called *Miacis*. Its remains have been found in rocks about 45 million years old, in Europe, Asia and North America, where it lived in the great forests which then stretched round most of the Northern Hemisphere. If you could bring the bones of *Miacis* to life, you would see an animal which seemed to have some of the characteristics of several, present-day families of carnivores. Indeed it is likely that apart from those of its descendants which became dogs, others evolved into weasels and raccoons and yet others into cats and hyaenas.

A carved mask of the jackal god Anubis — XIX or XX dynasty.

Certainly it would not look like a very promising ancestor for the dogs, for it was only about the size of a ferret, with a long sinuous body and heavy tail, and short but very flexible legs. The paws all had five, well formed toes and the feet would have looked much broader than those of a present-day dog, for the thumbs and great toes spread widely from the others, and could to some extent be folded back over the palms of the hands and the soles of the feet. This condition is called having opposable first toes, and any animal possessing it can hold things in the same manner as we do. It is almost always related to a tree-dwelling life, and there is little doubt that *Miacis* would have taken refuge from its enemies among the branches of its forest home. Its claws were retractile, like those of a cat, and would doubtless have helped it in climbing. It might have used its forefeet to some extent for holding its food, rather as a raccoon of today can, but if you could have watched *Miacis* eating, you would have noticed that it gulped down large chunks of meat which it sliced off the carcase of its prey, using teeth which were in the back of its mouth. These, which are called Carnassial teeth, shear

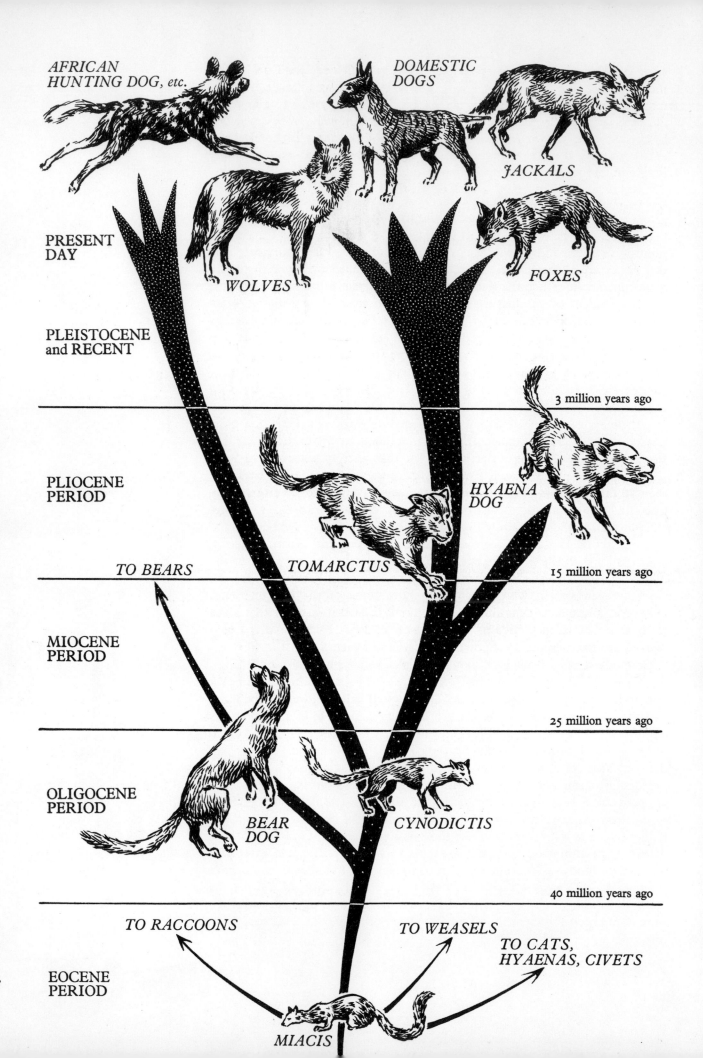

AFRICAN HUNTING DOG, etc.

DOMESTIC DOGS

JACKALS

PRESENT DAY

WOLVES

FOXES

PLEISTOCENE and RECENT

3 million years ago

PLIOCENE PERIOD

HYAENA DOG

TO BEARS

TOMARCTUS

15 million years ago

MIOCENE PERIOD

25 million years ago

OLIGOCENE PERIOD

BEAR DOG

CYNODICTIS

40 million years ago

TO RACCOONS

TO WEASELS

TO CATS, HYAENAS, CIVETS

EOCENE PERIOD

MIACIS

against each other like scissor blades. They are well developed in dogs of today, which feed like *Miacis* must have done. Hunting animals must be more knowing than the animals that they prey on or they will be outwitted. Had you been able to watch *Miacis* hunting, you might well have been struck by the cleverness of the animal, for although it was nothing like so clever as a dog of today it had a larger and more complex brain than any carnivore before it, and was probably quite intelligent.

The descendants of *Miacis* which began the developments culminating in the dogs, became ground livers, and although they may, at first, have remained in the cover of the forests, they were no longer climbers. At this point the family tree of the dog-like animals begins to become more complicated for some of them developed into heavyweights, becoming more massive and lumbering as time went on, until eventually the bears evolved from them. A more important descendant, although not the first of the dogs, is an animal called *Cynodictis*, which is fairly well known from fossils found in America. A little bigger than *Miacis*, it still had a long body and short limbs, but the claws on the toes were less fully retractile, and in the forelimb some of the bones of the wrist had become fused. This reduced the flexibility of the hand, but gave more rigidity to the limb for running. From *Cynodictis* all the true running dogs evolved, although the family tree branches again at this point, one division leading to the hunting dog of Africa and its relatives, the other to the true dogs. Although the two halves of the family look so alike, their separate descent can be traced back some 30 million years. Later the 'true dogs' branch divided again, part of it giving rise to some animals called hyaena-dogs, which were bone eating scavengers, and which for a short time in North America paralleled the hyaena of the Old World. The present day true dogs can be traced back to an animal called *Tomarctus*,

Left The evolution of the dog.

which lived about 20 million years ago. This creature was a plains dweller, preying on the game animals which at that time had become extremely numerous, following the first widespread development of grasses over much of the world. Along with the herbivores, predators also evolved, and *Tomarctus* was one of them. It was extremely doglike in its general appearance, although doubtless its intelligence and social life were not up to the standard of modern dogs. The wolves, the jackals and the foxes, the true wild dogs of today, are the distant, but not very different descendants of *Tomarctus*. Perhaps because they are structurally primitive great variation seems possible on the dog 'theme'. There are many races and forms of wild dog. In domestication this plasticity of the species continues, and many different strains have arisen, some of which would be quite unable to survive in the wild, but which have been perpetuated by breeders.

There is no doubt that the dog was the first animal to have been domesticated

Part of an Assyrian relief called 'The Hunt of Asshurbanipal' depicting hunting dogs pulling down a wild ass.

by man. The origins of domestication must lie far back in the Palaeolithic Period, before the end of the Pleistocene Ice Age. At this time, some 10,000 to 15,000 years ago man was a successful hunting animal, who must have competed for prey with the wolves and other dogs which lived in the same environment. But where, when, and even which of the many species of dog-like animals may have been involved, is something about which there is no agreement, although an Asiatic form, called the Pale-footed Wolf seems to be most like the earliest dogs.

There are many possible ways that the first domestication may have taken place. It is probable that the wolves were attracted to human camps by the vast quantities of meat which the primitive hunters must have wasted in times of plenty. The huge middens of their food debris were sometimes composed of the remains of tens of thousands of animals. The smell must have been overpowering, but to the wolves highly attractive, and a loose relationship must have arisen, with the wolves benefiting from the wastefulness of the humans, who in turn gained from the scavenging activities of

A maned wolf, from South America.

the wolves, although they may not have realized it. There must have been much suspicion on both sides, but probably neither side would normally attack the other, the wolves because human flesh is not their natural food, and the humans leaving them alone as long as easier prey was available.

How the first close relationship arose has been the subject of many flights of fancy. It is possible that young wolf cubs were occasionally fostered as pets particularly by children of the tribe. This sometimes happens today in Australia, when Aborigines adopt dingo puppies. These usually retreat to the wild as they grow up, but in many ways their fear of man is lessened. One can imagine semi-tame wolves, similarly brought up, joining in the hunt with men, helping to drive and stampede herds of game. Man would soon see the value of an animal with such speed, cunning and endurance, and make the first conscious effort to use the wolf as a hunting partner. It is probable that this occurred in many places, over a long span of time, involving a number of different, but closely related members of the wolf species, *Canis lupus*, with perhaps the Asiatic jackal being tamed occasionally.

An Australian dingo

A saddle-back or black-backed jackal, which is found in many parts of Africa, south of the Sahara.

In the wild this does not interbreed with the wolf species, which it overlaps in distribution, but in captivity it will certainly breed with domestic dogs, forming fertile hybrids, an indication of their extremely close relationship.

Once the ecological barrier had been broken in the hunters' camps, it is likely that jackals could have interbred with wolves. Some workers claim that some modern breeds of dog carry a strong dash of jackal, but generally wolf blood seems to be predominant. The more tractable animals would tend to stay with the humans, the wilder ones would run away. So semi-tame wolves would live round the camp, perhaps being restrained by man as their usefulness became more fully understood. Probably the weaker animals were selected as these would be easier to control. It seems as though this eventually led to the development of dogs like the pariahs and dingos, which appear to have many characteristics in common with those of some of the dogs found in early archaeological sites. Occasionally very small pups would be born to these captives, and kept, perhaps for food. We have, from Mesolithic sites in Denmark, dating back to 8,000 BC, remains of two types of dog, one large and one small. Even the large one was considerably smaller than the local race of wolves, and it has been suggested from this that the dogs had been imported from a more southerly region, where the original wolf stock was of smaller build. However, these dogs were probably mated with the large northern race of wolves, subsequently giving rise to a group of large dogs, presumably used for guarding purposes. The small dogs seem to have been house dogs, for they have been found, for example, in the Swiss lake dwellings, of a somewhat later date. During the European Bronze Age, about 2,000 BC, two other distinctive forms seem to have arisen. One was a smallish dog, roughly comparable to a Border Collie in size, and probably used for working sheep, which were becoming increasingly important at that time. The other was a medium-sized dog, which seems to have been

Statue of an ancient Egyptian
hunting dog.

Part of an Assyrian relief called 'The Hunt of Asshurbanipal', depicting attendants with dogs and hunting nets.

Two Salukis, members of the greyhound family. Of the purest descent, Salukis trace back to about 5,000 years ago, when they were little different from the dogs of today.

hound-like in some respects, and may have been used for hunting.

By earliest historic times these four basic types of dog seem to have given rise to many breeds. The Egyptians had a number, including Greyhound-like dogs, with curly tails. The Assyrians had mastiff-like breeds, which were used for hunting and for war. Some different breeds were developed in the Far East; these often seem to have been selected because of skull deformation and had short faces. Generally, however, the development of new breeds must have been slow, and maintaining a pure strain difficult. There are very few breeds of dog of the present day which can claim an unbroken ancestry to the earliest days of human civilization. The Saluki seems to be one, for it is very similar to some long-haired Greyhounds prized by the Ancient Egyptians. The majority of breeds can be traced back a few hundreds of years at the most, although today, with the science of genetics applied to dog breeding, many breeds are changing extremely rapidly. New breeds, such as the Dobermann Pinscher, have been developed and standardized in less than a hundred years. Others, such as some of the terriers, have changed almost beyond recognition in the last half century. These changes will probably continue to be made in many cases; a reminder of the primitive flexibility, both physical and mental, which continues to be an important part of the make-up of our dogs today.

DOGS IN MYTHOLOGY 2

In ancient Egypt life depended on the Nile. In a land scorched by the sun, and composed largely of harsh and stony soil, the rising of the river each year was the sign of returning life. The great river began to rise at the beginning of summer, and when the Egyptians judged the water to be at its height, in early August, the dykes were opened and the rich, life-giving water, thick with new soil, poured over the parched earth. The people depended on the Nile waters for their very life, though they never knew of the mountains of Ethiopia, or the mighty Lake Victoria. Irrigation was extensively practised and oases formed the basis of fixed settlements.

But sometimes the Nile failed to rise, and famine followed. The desert, never far from the cultivable land along the river, would encroach upon the outlying settlements, and the sun would set in the burning sky to the howling of an animal that belonged to the cruel wastes in the west. The jackal was a creature despised in life and feared after death; it was cowardly and slunk around stealing its food—and it despoiled the dead, a terrible thing to a people who believed so fervently in the afterlife.

It was these very circumstances which, paradoxically, made a god of the despised desert dog, and it may well represent the point in history when the dog entered mythology. The early religion of the Egyptians grew more sophisticated as the great civilization developed. The desolate waste of sand was where the solar barque disappeared from the sky—into death, to be reborn the following day on the eastern horizon. So the west became the land of the dead, and it is for this reason that most of the great kings built their tombs on the left bank of the Nile on the edge of the desert. The jackal came from there—a messenger from the other world.

The memory of the grave-despoiling creature remained with the people of Egypt, and when the Pharaoh himself was buried the vestiges of this fear could be seen in the funeral rites. The jackal was at first represented by a priest wearing an appropriate mask. But time went by and the kings of Egypt came to be regarded as gods on earth, and when a god was conducted to the presence of Osiris who should be his guide? Another god, obviously, and the connection remained firm. The creature from the desert underwent a metamorphosis, and there was no more need for a priest to wear a mask. The god Anubis, with his jackal's head, took his place in the pantheon and became the conductor of souls.

There is what seems an odd parallel with Anubis in the Norse association of the wolf with the leader of the gods, Odin. His creatures were the wolf and the raven, both of them scavengers who feasted on the dead. But the parallel is less odd when one remembers that Odin was, among other things, a god of the dead. Both ravens and wolves turn up frequently in stories of war and valour in Old Norse and Old English literature, though their part is not a heroic one.

The wolf in fact plays an equivocal part in the Norse myths. His place as a creature of death is at the side of Odin, but it is a wolf who will be Odin's last foe at *Ragnarok*, the time when the gods meet their doom. They will fight valiantly: Thor will go forth against the serpent coiled around the world, and Odin will meet Fenrir, the great grey wolf who is the son of

The dead Cuchulain. The Irish hero's invicibility was overcome by the use of a dog in a ceremony performed by three witches to bring about his death. In Celtic mythology the dog is often portrayed as the creature of death.

An Egyptian statue of the Saïte period, showing the jackal-headed Anubis, the god who conducted the souls of the dead to the presence of Osiris to be judged.

A model of a dog in terra-cotta from Mexico, 3rd century AD. This fat, little dog represents a creature often cherished in pre-Columbian Mexico, and even endowed with a degree of divinity. But it was cherished and spoiled because it was eventually eaten.

Colour
Irish Wolfhound

Loki, the strange dark god who seems to epitomize the dark side of man's nature and, ultimately, his leaning towards self-destruction. Odin will be devoured by Fenrir, and Thor will die of the venom of the serpent. The gods will meet their inescapable doom — the *wyrd* which was the portion of every man. Even the god of death had to meet the creature of death.

In African myth there is the story of the dog who actually brought death to mankind. The Mende people of Sierra Leone tell how the Supreme Being made two animals the vehicle of his will. He sent out two messengers, a dog and a toad. The dog's message was that man would be immortal, while the toad's message was that man would die. They set out together, and on the way they passed a woman who was preparing food for her child. The dog sat down and waited, and did in fact get some of the food for himself. Then he rose and hurried after the toad. But he had dallied too long and the toad reached mankind first. So the message that came was that man would die.

IRISH
WOLFHOUND

IRISH
WOLFHOUND

The most familiar dog in classical mythology is in fact the wolf. Apollo himself, among his other descriptions, was called *Lycian* Apollo, and the sacred creature of Mars was also the wolf. The Romans held a feast on the 15th of every February called the Lupercalia, a fertility festival but with details in its performance that suggest the propitiation of a wolf spirit. The festival's origins were very ancient and looked back to the time when Rome was a pastoral community and wolves were much feared. Both Mars and Apollo were originally shepherd gods, and Mars was accredited with the siring of Romulus and Remus—a myth which is probably a confusion of the original character of Mars with the Romans' desire to ascribe their ancestry to a god that they, as warriors, particularly revered.

In its most familiar form the story tells of Numitor, the king of Alba Longa, a city in the hills of Latium. He was deposed by his younger brother, Amulius, who was careful to remove any possibility of the throne being reclaimed by any son of the lawful line. He placed Numitor's daughter, Rhea Silvia, with the Vestal Virgins to keep her from the sight of men; but she was violated by Mars himself, and bore twin sons.

Amulius imprisoned the unhappy mother and threw the babies into the Tiber, at that time in flood. The cradle containing the twins drifted ashore and was found by a she-wolf, who suckled the children until they were found and cared for by one of the royal shepherds. The children grew up big and strong—as the children of Mars would—and after killing Amulius and restoring the throne to Numitor they went on to found the city of Rome.

The story, apart from its function as a myth of origins, bears the same stamp as the evolution of Anubis into a god: the wolf and the jackal were creatures to be feared, so they were propitiated, and found their way into the company of the gods. The domestic dog, which is a descendant of all wild dogs, has on the other hand been badly served by the creature who

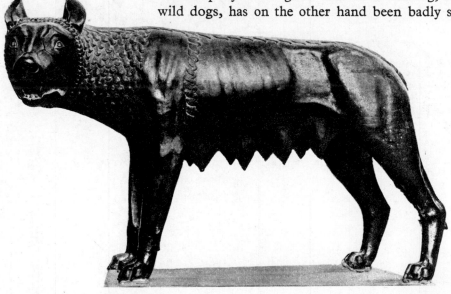

The she-wolf of the Capitol. This remarkable Etruscan bronze is often shown accompanied by twin babies representing Romulus and Remus. But only the she-wolf is authentic — the figures of the twins are of a much later period.

owes him most. It may be that race memory is too persistent, that the dog has been too much associated with death. His howling announced its presence and he was known to be a scavenger. He is honoured enough now—too much, in some respects—but the age of myth is always the day before yesterday, and plainly men thought differently then. Perhaps his very familiarity with man kept him from achieving divine status, though as a creature that *serves* his place in myth is secure.

III.

When Odysseus returned to his palace from his long wanderings after the fall of Troy he was nearly savaged by the dogs to whom he was a stranger. But the old hound lying abandoned in the dung heap, recognized him and had just strength enough for a last, hopeful wag of his tail before he died. The old hound, Argus, was almost the only likeable character in the famous epic, where so much of the story is taken up with revenge and bloodshed.

The return of Odysseus. This 19th century painting captures the pathos of the last meeting between the hero — unrecognized at his palace gate — and Argus, the old hound which was the only creature which knew him.

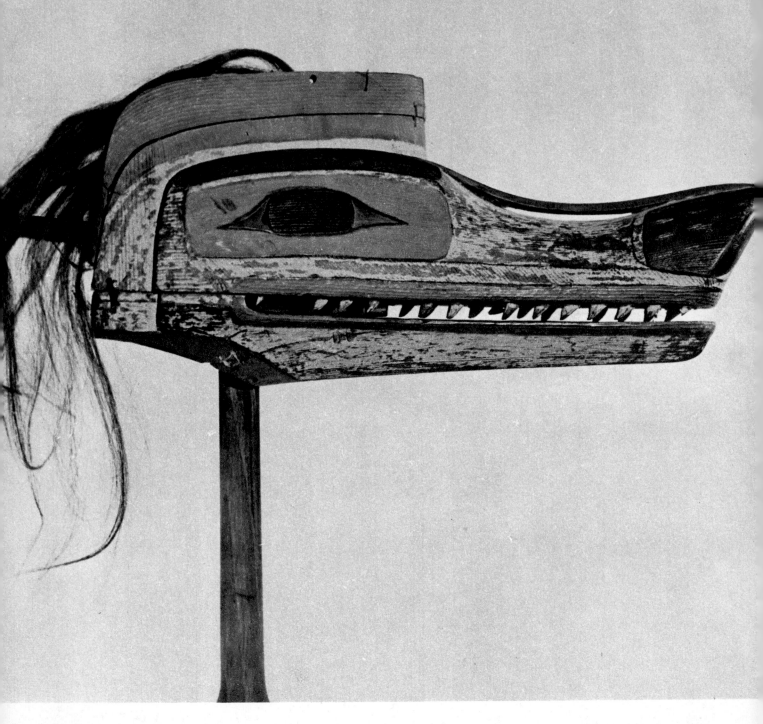

A dance mask representing a wolf's head from the north-west coast Red Indians of Nootka Sound. The Indians of the plains and the south-east made friends with the dog, but its most familiar form in the Pacific north-west was the wolf, which remained their feared and dangerous enemy.

Among the Mandan Indians of the great American prairie the partnership of man and dog is explained by the encounter between the first two creatures on earth. One was Lone Man, and one day he met another creature who called himself First Man. Soon after meeting they began to fight about precedence, and Lone Man succeeded in killing First Man. The body of First Man quickly became a skeleton, and while Lone Man was regarding it with satisfaction a movement of his spear made the bones click. The clicking continued and First Man stood up, completely restored. So the two decided to hunt together. The creature who called himself First Man was Coyote.

In a different region of North America, the south-eastern states, a myth survives of the Natchez Indians, which tells of the dog who warned Man of an impending deluge. He counselled Man to make a raft, which lifted him to safety while everything else was drowned. The dog told him next that he would have to return to the place of his origin, and explained that Man would have to throw him, the dog, into the flood to make this possible. Man, torn between his feeling for his companion and his trust in his counsel, brought himself at length to push the dog into the waters—which immediately began to subside. The dog's last advice to Man was that he must not leave the raft until seven days had gone by, when the earth would have completely dried. And seven days after the flood, sitting by the fire on his raft, Man saw people approaching him; some naked, some ragged, and some richly dressed. The three groups divided the fire between them, and then an Old Man, or spirit, appeared from the East. He told Man that the strangers were dead, but would continue to live in spirit.

The myth is puzzling, not least because the part of the dog in the story is so strange. He is plainly the creature who serves, and it may be that this is his only function; but there is a strong suggestion of a bond in the past, which no doubt receded from memory as the Natchez began to live in more organized communities.

China, the country of the marvellous and misrepresented Pekinese dogs, is also the country of a charming story about a dog that married a princess.

The Red Indians of the American plains made good use of the dog. It was often used for food, and sometimes made an excellent beast of burden to haul goods along, rather like the Husky of the Eskimo.

The Jung tribesmen of Fuchow tell of him; he belonged to one of the Emperor's generals, and during a war which was going badly for China, overheard the Emperor declare that he would give his daughter in marriage, to whomever was courageous enough to bring him the enemy chief's head. The Emperor was well aware that the chief was the strength of the enemy army, and he hoped that this stratagem would demoralize them.

The dog listened carefully to the discussion of the Emperor's declaration, and learned that no one in the Chinese camp felt brave enough to make the attempt. So that night he left the camp and slipped through the enemy lines. He found the chief asleep in his tent, and gnawed off his head, and carried the trophy back to the Chinese camp, where he haid it at the Emperor's feet.

The Emperor's strategy worked: the enemy found their chief's headless body and, without a leader, fled from the scene. There was much rejoicing, and the dog now came forward and reminded the Emperor of his promise. The Emperor, confounded, explained to the dog that there could not possibly be a marriage between a woman and a dog; the dog replied that he would,

A terra-cotta dog from a tomb of the Han Dynasty (China, 3rd century AD). The dog which married a princess was more likely to have been ordinary-looking like this dog rather than an aristocrat of the Emperor's court.

24

in that case, turn himself into a man. He would lie under a bell for the space of 280 days, and then he would be ready for his wedding. (It should be mentioned that bells in China were not merely something to ring; they were used in ritual from the earliest recorded period, and were regarded as possessing sacred qualities.)

After 279 days had passed the Emperor, overcome with curiosity, lifted the bell and looked under the rim. His rashness broke the spell, and he was confronted with a young man who wore a dog's head—the remaining day would have seen the transformation completed. But the imperial promise was kept, and the princess was solemnly married to a brave young man who, strangely, wore a thick red veil over his head for the ceremony.

The marriage was fruitful, but the children were all like their father, and to this day the Jung tribesmen wear red coverings over their faces. They also paint the figure of a dog on their screens to celebrate the old-style New Year, thus honouring their brave ancestor who defeated China's foes.

From another eastern country rich in mythology, India, comes one of the

Pekinese on a painted silk scroll. These marvellous dogs, it was said, were born from the Emperor's wish for a dog which was brave and beautiful — and small enough to lie in the Emperor's sleeve.

The five Pandava princes set out
for Indra's heaven on Mount
Meru. King Yudhisthira leads
the little group, followed by
Bhima, Arjuna, Nakula, Sahadeva;
and Draupadi, who was Queen
and wife to all the brothers. The
dog who joined them from
nowhere, as they left their city of
Hastinapur, was the only creature
who reached Meru with
Yudhisthira. From an Indian
manuscript in the British Museum.

most touching of all stories about a man and his dog. It occurs at the end of
the *Mahabharata*, the monumental epic of the Hindus which is longer than
the *Iliad* and the *Odyssey* combined. King Yudhisthira, secure on the throne
of Hastinapur after cruel and exhausting wars, is saddened to hear of the
death of his late adversaries, the Kauravas, in a fire in the forest to which they
had retired after acknowledging the victory of Yudhisthira and his Pandava
brothers. Yudhisthira was an upright man and had no ill-will for his erst-
while enemies. Soon after this came the news that Krishna, the glorious
friend of all the Pandavas' exploits, was dead also, and the king decided that
he was weary of this life. He determined to set out for Mount Meru, where
lay Indra's heaven, and when he told his brothers they agreed to accompany
him—they would rather leave the world together than be separated. Draupadi,
who was wife to all five brothers, decided that she would go too.

So the five brothers and their wife set out from Hastinapur, and a dog
followed them from the city, trotting along behind them all the way into the
mountains. It was on the first slopes of the Himalayas that the first one died.
It was Draupadi, the wife, and Bhima, the strongest of the brothers, asked
the king why this should be—why should Draupadi die so far from Indra's
heaven? Yudhisthira replied that she was guilty of loving one brother—
Arjuna—more than the others. They went on, and then one of the brothers
fell, Sahadeva, Bhima asked the same question, and the king told him that
Sahadeva was vain of his wisdom, believing himself wiser than all other men.

The other brothers began to die, one by one, and Yudhisthira had to
answer Bhima's anguished question: 'Why should they die now—when we
are so far from our journey's end?' The king explained: the beautiful Nakula
fell because he was vain of his handsomeness, and Arjuna, the valiant and
heroic Arjuna, because he was contemptuous of his foes. Then Bhima
himself began to weaken; he dragged himself along until he could move no
farther, and cried out in despair to his brother to tell him why. Yudhisthira
told him that he boasted too much of his great size and strength.

Now Yudhisthira was alone on the mountainside, his wife and brothers

dead. He trudged on wearily, his heart heavy, and then found that he did, after all, have a companion. The dog was still trotting by his side as he went higher and deeper into the mountains in his quest for Mount Meru.

One exhausted man and one tired, panting dog arrived at heaven's gate. Indra, king of the gods, came forth in his chariot and welcomed Yudhisthira, telling him to mount the chariot and be carried into heaven. The exhausted king told him that his wife and brothers had died on the journey, and what was heaven to him without those he loved? Indra told him to take heart, that they were in heaven already and he would be reunited with them. Yudhisthira, reassured, called his dog only to be told that there was no place for dogs in heaven. He protested—the dog had been his only friend when he would have died of grief and weariness. Indra told him not to be concerned, that he was about to join the ranks of the immortals. What was a dog to him? Yudhisthira told the king of the gods that the dead were dead, and could not be brought back to life—that was why he had continued to climb when his wife and brothers died. He had never forsaken them while they lived, and the dog had remained his friend throughout the long and bitter journey. He would not forsake the faithful creature now.

Then the dog began to change. Yudhisthira saw him become a radiant and noble man, a celestial figure in no way diminished by the presence of Indra. The stranger spoke: 'I am Dharma—your mortal and spiritual duty, righteousness. And I am your father, who was testing you. Now you are seen to have compassion for all living things. We will mount Indra's chariot together, and pass through heaven's gate.'

IV.

One might wonder, after reading that story, about the lot of dogs in India today, where most of them are despised, ill-used, starved and generally rejected. But then, the story of the compassionate king and his faithful dog belongs to myth and the age of myth is always the day before yesterday.

3 FARM DOGS

In its long history as a servant of man there can be little doubt that the most useful of all dogs has been and still is the sheepdog, in its various forms. Without sheepdogs the production of mutton would be an uneconomic proposition in Great Britain, Australia, New Zealand, U.S.S.R. and many other countries where sheep are kept intensively.

Many different types and breeds have been evolved, suited to the wide variety of conditions under which they work. In some countries sheepdogs are kept to guard the flocks not to herd them. In the British Isles sheepdogs are expected to help the shepherd to herd his flocks. Practically all the true herding sheepdogs in the world today stem from British stock. The Australian Kelpie (a Scottish word for water nymph) is no more than a strain produced by mixing various types of British dogs (with the possible but improbable inclusion of Dingo blood) and carefully breeding to produce a dog suited to local conditions. Likewise the Australian Cattle Dog has been evolved for a specific purpose, and this time there seems little doubt that the Dingo has played an important part in its evolution. The sheepdogs of New Zealand seem no different from those in our own country and there are probably more 'Beardies' in that country than in their native Scotland today.

In Britain there are several breeds of sheep and cattle dogs with many

Three Border Collies on an English farm.

Sheep-farming in New Zealand. Sometimes riding and sometimes on foot the musterer gathers up small 'mobs' of sheep round the wind-swept ridges. They are driven down to the lower levels fo form part of the full muster of the block.

A Maori shepherd with his dogs. On the larger hill-country stations in New Zealand a shepherd usually has five or six dogs, consisting of 'huntaways', a 'heading' dog and a 'handy' dog. The 'huntaways' are noisy, driving dogs, which rely on a loud and frequent bark to move sheep. The 'heading' dog is used to bring the sheep up to the shepherd and hold them in one spot. The 'handy' dog, a combination of the other types, can both head and hunt, and is generally very versatile.

types to be found in each breed. This often gives rise to the idea that they are all mongrels. Many people have the idea that to be pure-bred a dog must have a pedigree written on a piece of paper. But pieces of paper make no difference to dogs and have little influence on most shepherds. No shepherd would ever mate his bitch to anything but the best dog he could find—a system adhered to from generation to generation which has resulted in sheepdogs being amongst the purest of all breeds found in the British Isles.

Different types have evolved to suit different types of work and different types of country in which that work is carried out. On the heather clad, rock strewn hills of some of Scotland and amongst the hills of the English Lake District, big strong dogs are necessary. Built more on the lines of a Lurcher than on the conventional idea of a sheepdog these are known as 'wearing' dogs, which instinctively run out round the flock and turn it back to the shepherd. They will go out a mile or more to gather all the sheep on a hillside and 'wear' them quietly to the shepherd, who need not have moved from the glen below. If he moves on the dog will keep all the sheep following behind.

In some parts, particularly in the Western Highlands much of the ground is covered with bracken, which, combined with the deep gullies, known as

Two Border Collies rounding up a flock of Blackface sheep on the mountains in Wales.

corries, makes it impossible for the above type of dog to see his sheep or the sheep to see him. Here the shepherd has to get out above the sheep and more or less chase them out of the thick cover with dogs known as 'hunters'. These are noisy dogs which work across the hill in front of the shepherd, barking almost incessantly. Even if the dog and sheep do not see each other the latter will soon run from the sound of the barking. Once out in the open the shepherd will probably call the 'hunter' back to heel and finish the journey with a 'wearer'.

Hunters are not so carefully bred as wearers and their working is much more rough and ready. Although of little use to gather a big hillside most of these dogs will wear at hand. That is to say they will gather a bunch of sheep in a field or turn them on the road. This type of dog was used extensively as a drover's dog with sheep and cattle in the days before motor transport. Many are still to be found in the markets of the big stockbreeding areas, forcing sheep and cattle into pens and trucks. The Bearded Collie which has been recognized by the Kennel Club, and is therefore seen at dog shows, has always been popular in Scotland for this type of work.

In was also to be found on the dairy and mixed farms of the Scottish lowlands, but much more common was the old fashioned Scotch Collie, at

The sheepdog has guided the shepherd to where a lost lamb lies hidden in a drain, and still alive, the shepherd pulls it out.

The Collie's name is derived from the colley or mountain sheep of the Scottish Highlands where it was used to work these sheep. Because of its remarkable utility and intelligence it is still used for handling large flocks and is extremely popular in Australia for this reason.

one time found all over Scotland and England. A big handsome dog, usually tricolour or sable with a heavy coat, this type was rarely an outstanding worker but nevertheless an excellent all-rounder. From this type of dog the modern show collie has been developed. It is hard to believe that from a dog with a broad head, well defined stop and big bold eyes looking straight ahead, man has produced a freak with a long narrow head, no stop at all, with little furtive eyes set on either side of the skull. Even sadder is the fact that the original has become practically extinct except in Ireland. There one can see many dogs of this type, probably descended from stock taken there by the cattle and horse dealers who have always travelled regularly between Scotland and Ireland.

In the south of England sheep used to be folded on arable crops instead of being run extensively on grass. Here the 'Bobtail' was used almost universally. The show version of this is the Old English Sheepdog which bears more resemblance to a sheep than a dog and many people may wonder how such a dog could work sheep. The answer is that it could not. This type of dog is still quite common on farms right along the south of England from Hampshire to Cornwall, although they are now rarely seen in Kent or Sussex. In Dorset they are known as Dorset Shags, but they are all really the same breed. They have nothing like the coat of the specimens seen on the benches at Crufts dog show or advertising paint on television commercials. And what coat they do have is shorn every year at shearing time. As a folded flock would rarely occupy more than an acre or two at a time the dog never had to cover great distances, but in winter he often worked knee deep in mud for weeks or months on end. One would expect the heavy coat to be a big handicap under such circumstances. Nevertheless I have been assured by several old shepherds who have compared various types that the Bobtail is the only one which can stand up to this work for any length of time.

In East Anglia there are Smithfield dogs, produced by crossing collies from Scotland with native Bobtails. They were popular with the drovers who

An Old English Sheepdog or Bobtail. This dog is easily the largest of British sheepdogs but is now rarely used as a worker. Its wool is often spun and woven to make clothes.

A German shepherd with a Bearded Collie watching his sheep in Bavaria.

Sheep-droving in New Zealand. This mob of sheep numbers 2,800 and is being handled by two drovers and several dogs on a journey which will take about ten weeks.

Sheep being rounded up and penned before being dipped in Cornwall.

Colour
Caucasian Sheepdog

Border Collie with ducks

Two Border Collies rounding up sheep at a Trial

Two German Short-haired Pointers

CAUCASIAN SHEEP DOG

BORDER COLLIE

GERMAN →

BORDER COLLIES

SHORTHAIR

HUNGARIAN KOMONDOR

HUNGARIAN KOMONDOR

used to drive sheep and cattle to London's Smithfield market — hence the name. These are still popular as workers and also for crossing with greyhounds to produce Norfolk Lurchers, so popular with gypsies everywhere. In appearance and style working Smithfield dogs are very similar to Scottish Beardies, the Welsh Greys and a similar type in Ireland. Shaggy dogs are in fact, to be found all over the world.

The Welsh Sheepdog, though similar in type to the collies of Scotland could never compare as a worker. Few could be trained to gather a mountainside (hills in Scotland — mountains in Wales) and they worked more on the lines of a hunter, driving the sheep ahead of the shepherd — not always where he wanted them either!

Wales also had its Corgis, famed not for their ability to work but for their popularity with the Royal Family. I bred Corgis (in Scotland!) before they gained such popularity through the Royal Family's love of them. And I worked them regularly on both sheep and cattle. Although not very good with sheep they simply had no equals as cattle dogs, and incidentally could hold their own as ratters with the best of terriers. These were Pembroke corgis, but in Wales today the Cardigan is more popular as a worker.

In the North of England one still finds Lancashire Heelers which look rather like long legged Corgis and work in exactly the same way. Whether these and the Corgis of Wales originated from the same ancestry or whether the Heelers are descended from Corgis taken to Lancashire it is difficult to say, but they are certainly very similar.

On the green hills of the Scottish/English border country were to be found 'strong-eyed' dogs or 'creepers'. Although they looked very much like any other collie these dogs worked in quite a different way from all the other 'loose-eyed' dogs which we have been discussing. With its 'eye'

Colour
A Hungarian Komondor

A Welsh Collie. This very adaptable type of sheepdog is well known in North Wales, and dogs of this breed have even been used by railway companies to free their lines from mountain sheep.

A sheepdog in the Border Fells accelerates madly to head off a sheep it has separated from the flock.

A good 'strong-eyed' dog will hold sheep motionless with its stare. Here a heading dog shows its skill by holding three sheep in New Zealand. It will not move till the next order comes from the shepherd.

a creeper can 'hold' a sheep. In other words the dog can fix the sheep to such an extent that it is practically hypnotized into standing still, moving to right or left or in any other direction the dog wants. Apart from this 'strong-eye' holding the sheep, it also keeps the dog back from a lot of sheep so that he does not fluster or panic them.

By now you may have noticed that I classify dogs according to how they work rather than how they look. This is because, unlike most people who write, I am a working dog man. And people who work dogs value them according to their ability to work and not according to their looks. That

is why type varies so much in working dogs, and also why working ability is so often lacking in show dogs.

You may also have noticed that I have made no reference at all to sheepdog trials or to the Border Collies to be seen working at them. That is because I have been dealing with the past rather than the present, and both sheepdog trials and the dogs seen at them are comparatively new innovations.

As to sheepdog trials, the first record of a sheepdog trial was of one held in Wales in 1873 which was won by a Scotsman with a strong-eyed dog. This was no doubt the start of the great invasion of Wales by this type of dog, now known as the Border Collie. So much so that many people assume that it is native to the English/Welsh border and it is even referred to on occasion as a Welsh Collie. The fact is that it has completely ousted the native Welsh Sheepdog and even today the majority of Welsh winners in sheepdog trials are either imported from Scotland or bred from imported stock.

Sheepdog trials soon became popular in the whole of the British Isles and, as they did, so the demand for strong-eyed dogs, which could win at them, increased. In 1910 the International Sheepdog Society was formed and published its first stud book. And so started a revolution in the breeding and working of sheepdogs throughout the British Isles and the sheep-raising countries of the world. Sheepdog trials soon became popular with the general public, enabling them to be run at a profit. This in turn meant that more and more were held at which shepherds could see just what could be achieved by a well bred, well trained dog. Many of them would either buy a Border Collie pup or mate one of their own local strain bitches to a trial winner. As a result it is now practically impossible to find any of the old fashioned types of sheepdog in its pure form.

Although some of the pedigrees go back over fifty years and very close inbreeding has been practised, type is very varied in Border Collies. The

On this farm in Devon it is a problem to prevent the sheep straying from the moors on to the main road. Although a cattle-grid was placed across the road it still did not have the desired effect. So the farmer had to post two dogs on permanent guard duty to hold them back.

Sheepdog trials held in Hyde Park, London.

A sheepdog rounding up sheep on a farm in Kent.

ability to work is all that matters to breeders. The form of entry for the International Sheepdog Society stud book has a space for size: — 'large, medium or small' and one for coat: — 'rough coated, medium coated, smooth coated or beardie'. And there is no colour bar. Black and white predominates, followed by tricolour (black, tan and white), but registered pups turn up blue merle, slate blue, sable or chocolate. Quite often all white pups turn up although they are very unpopular with shepherds because sheep do not 'respect' a white dog as they do a dark one, and lambs will usually run after it with apparent curiosity.

Sheepdog trials have long been popular in Australia, New Zealand and the U.S.A. and many other countries, and Border Collies are now to be found in every country in the world where sheep are herded. The breed's superiority as a worker is not due to superior intelligence, and from experience I would say that many other breeds of dog have a higher I.Q. Its superiority is due to its tremendous instinct to work — and to work in a certain way. A 'wide-run, strong-eyed' dog can control a flock of sheep with a quiet efficiency unknown in any other breed. The Border Collie could be described as the classic sheepdog but it is worth remembering that the instinct which puts him above all other dogs stems from the wild dog's instinct to stalk and hunt his prey, and there is no question of any 'almost human' affection for sheep as some people appear to think.

4 TOY DOGS IN ART

The fourth Duke and Duchess of Marlborough with their family, by Sir Joshua Reynolds, (Blenheim Palace). In this picture can be seen two toy spaniels, one a Cavalier King Charles and the other either a Papillon or a Cavalier. In the foreground there is a nice example of an Italian Greyhound.

In case the title may suggest this is for highbrows, it should be made clear right at the outset that this is a study which can bring endless pleasure and interest to dog-lovers of all ages, and for a variety of reasons. And, in pursuing this interest, the devotee acquires, more or less as a bonus issue, an acquaintance with all the treasures of the artistic beauty of the past.

The reason why toy dogs figure so prominently in art, over the centuries, is not far to seek. From time immemorial, the ladies in households of consequence, have owned their toy dogs, and have taken the greatest pride in these decorative pets. What more natural, therefore, than that they should insist on these constant companions being included in the family portraits? In fact, in a number of cases where a family was painted more than once, either by the same artist or by more than one, it is possible to establish that they not only portray the same people, but also the same dogs.

Another possible reason why toy dogs figure so often and so prominently in pictures may be that the artist himself may have been a particular admirer of one or other of the toy breeds, or indeed may have owned one. In such

a case, it may have been at his instigation that the dogs were included in the finished composition, and it may even be that he painted in his own dogs. As a possible instance one can take the case of the famous Flemish artist, Peter Paul Rubens. Toy spaniels figure prominently in a great number of his masterpieces. He was an artist who painted his dogs with great care and accuracy, even when they did not form a major part of the work as a whole. Moreover, there is a painting in Stockholm, entitled 'Rubens' Drawing Room' in which there is a dog, presumably the property of the Rubens family, which appears to be a toy spaniel. The painter, or painters, of this picture are not known for certain. It is believed to be a composite painting by Van Dyck and Cornelis de Vos. Whoever the artist, however, the dog was not painted with anything like the care taken by Rubens over his dog subjects, and its identification is therefore uncertain. Nonetheless, it is not beyond the bounds of possibility, that the Rubens family toy dog may have been used as the 'model' for some of those figuring in his paintings.

There are sixteen toy breeds in Britain at the present time, of which fifteen are represented in moderate to large numbers, and are recognized by the Kennel Club. Of these, some are of fairly recent origin, produced and refined by selective interbreeding of more than one other breed, and so do not figure significantly in the world of art. Others, such as the popular Pekinese and the Smooth Coat Chihuahua, are of comparatively recent introduction, and come from countries where they cannot readily be traced through art channels. But of the remainder, there are seven which figure consistently in European art over several centuries, and with varying degrees of frequency, and to which therefore, this chapter is devoted.

'Miss Bowles' by Sir Joshua Reynolds, (Wallace Collection London). She is holding a King Charles Spaniel.

Statuette of miniature Greyhounds
at play, 1st century BC, (British
Museum).

When man first hunted for his livelihood, and for sport, the only weapons at his disposal to kill his prey were knives, clubs and spears. In consequence, his hounds were trained to chase and pull down the quarry which was too fleet of foot for him to catch unaided. It is natural, therefore, that the first minature breed we find in ancient art is the Italian Greyhound.

These beautiful little dogs, which should not be confused with the Whippet, from which breed they differ in a number of respects, have existed, virtually unchanged, for several thousand years. They are thought to have existed in Egypt as far back as 5,000 BC, and a skeleton of a small greyhound, which has been dated at about 3,000 BC has been dug up in that country. Coming forward a little, they certainly figure in numbers of tablets, reliefs on ceramics and in statues of Roman and Greek Art from the 6th century BC. A fine example, is the statuette in the British Museum of Miniature Greyhounds at Play, of Roman origin, and dated first century BC.

Paintings in which dogs can be positively identified first appear around the 12th/13th centuries AD. Of more than usual interest, in that it shows that up to the 15th century, and despite their small size, these dogs were still used for hunting, is the painting by Paolo Uccello (1396—1477) of The Hunt in the Forest (Ashmolean, Oxford).

That they had progressed beyond the frontiers of Italy by the 14th century is indicated by a German painting of that period in Karlsruhe, and

'The Hunt in the Forest' by Paolo Uccello, (Ashmolean Museum, Oxford). Miniature Greyhounds were still being used for hunting in the 15th century.

48

into France in the 15th century in a painting by Roger van der Weyden of King Phillip the Good, as also one of King Francis I by an unknown artist. By the 17th century they had crossed the Channel to England, and one figures in a portrait of the Merry Monarch — King Charles II — by Sir Peter Lely (1618—1680), though more interesting, perhaps, from a dog-lover's point of view, is the Royal Portrait in Hampton Court, by Van Somer, of Queen Anne with her dogs. By this time also, they had penetrated to Sweden, as is to be seen from the portrait by David Ehrenstrahl, entitled Fidelitas, dated 1678, and now in Stockholm.

In the 18th century came the development nowadays referred to as the Conversation Piece, consisting of groups — family or friends — carefully

Queen Anne of Denmark by Van Somer, (Hampton Court), with her miniature Greyhounds.

'Portrait of a Fishing Party' by William Hogarth, (Dulwich College Picture Gallery), showing an Italian Greyhound.

posed in indoor or rural settings, and often with their pets. This period is a real hunting ground for those seeking pictures in which their favourite breed may figure, and we find Italian Greyhounds in many of them. William Hogarth (1697—1764), who has been called the originator of this type of composition, has one in his portrait of a Fishing Party (Dulwich Gallery).

Others of this type and period include Pietro Longhi's (1702—1785) Family at Home (Venice), Angelica Kauffmann's (1741—1807) King Ferdinand of the Two Sicilies with his Family (Naples), and Adolf Menzel's (1815—1905) Frederick the Great at Table (Berlin). With the advent of reliable bows and arrows, and as man became armed with weapons with which to shoot his game, he trained his dogs to seek out and retrieve his quarry, and so came the retrieving breeds, and their smaller relatives, the toy spaniels, of which three distinct breeds are recognized. These are the Cavalier King Charles Spaniel, the King Charles Spaniel, and the Papillon.

At this stage some explanation of the recent history of the two breeds of King Charles Spaniel becomes necessary. The King Charles Spaniel of today is a short faced breed, with a practically non-existent muzzle. It was not so originally, and the shorter face was bred into it during the 19th century. In the 1920s, an American visiting Britain saw the King Charles of that era, and with the aim of breeding back to the earlier type, offered a large prize, by the standards of those days, for a King Charles with the original longer fore-face. As a result this type was duly selectively bred, and acquired the name of Cavalier King Charles Spaniel. In fact, as can readily be seen from paintings of the past, the present day Cavalier King Charles Spaniel now resembles the King Charles of the days prior to the 19th century.

The Papillon is a smaller dog than the King Charles or the Cavalier, and differs markedly in outward appearance, in that it carries its tail over the back in a graceful arc. In fact, on the Continent at one time they were referred to as *chiens écureils* (squirrel dogs). They may have their ears either fully dropped, as in the other spaniels, or fully erect, and as such are the only spaniels which may have erect ears. In some countries abroad, the two varieties are separately classified, the erect — or more properly described, oblique-eared variety being called Papillon (butterfly) and the drop-eared version Phalène (moth). They are not recognized by the British Kennel Club as spaniels, despite the fact that on the Continent, from whence they originated, they have been so classified for centuries, and are to this day.

A further difference between the Papillon and the Cavalier is that the latter has a distinctly broader head and muzzle, this last in the Papillon

Cavalier King Charles Spaniel, King Charles Spaniel and a Papillon.

PAPILLON

being very fine, tapering towards the nose, and rather longer than in the Cavalier in proportion to the length of the skull.

In view of the foregoing, we shall consider only the longer faced version of the King Charles (and will refer to it throughout as the Cavalier) jointly with both versions of the Papillon, that is to say the drop- and oblique-eared varieties, since both breeds have a very close common history. In fact, though many paintings can be positively identified as being of one or other of these breeds, many could well be of either.

Evidence of the existence of the toy spaniel breeds as we know them today starts about the 13th century AD, in Central Italy. By the 15th century the type had been established and stabilized to the extent that there are many paintings of dogs which, were they alive today, could well be taken into the show ring and win prizes.

An early painting of exceptional beauty is that by Titian (died 1576) known as the Venus of Urbino (Uffizi Gallery, Florence), of Eleanora Gonzaga, Duchess of Urbino, with her red and white Papillon curled up on the divan at her feet. Of much the same era is that by Giorgio Vassari (1511—1577) of Lorenzo de Medici receiving the Ambassadors. This is the first evidence of a princely owner of a toy spaniel.

By this time, the Papillon had spread to France, as had also, doubtless, the larger Cavalier. They were at the Court of King Charles IX of France, as evidenced by François Clouet's (1510—1572) portrait of the King's sister, Marguerite de Valois, who later became the wife of King Henry IV. In fact, from this time onwards, we can trace toy spaniels at the Court of France in each and every reign right up to the Revolution, when Queen Marie Antoinette took her beloved Papillons with her into imprisonment, and even, so it is said, to the guillotine. Of these portraits, one which depicts a typical

King Charles Spaniels by Sir Edwin Landseer (Tate Gallery, London).

Previous page
'Louis XIV with his Heirs', by
Largillière, (Wallace Collection,
London). This portrait depicts
a typical Papillon.

'Pineapple Picture' by Henry
Danckerts, (Collection of the
Marchioness of Cholmondeley).
This picture, which is famous
because it shows King Charles II
presented with the first pineapple
grown in England, portrays two
of the Spaniels, which were named
after him.

Colour

'Vanity' by Memling, (Strasbourg
Museum). Here are a Maltese
and an Italian Greyhound.

Detail from 'King Ferdinand of the
Two Sicilies with his family'
by Angelica Kauffman, (Museum
of Naples).

'The Venus of Urbino' by Titian,
(Uffizi Gallery, Florence). A red
and white Papillon is curled up at
her feet.

Papillon is that by Largillière (1656—1746) of Louis XIV with his Heirs, in the Wallace Collection. Another in the same collection, is the portrait of singular beauty of Madame de Pompadour, perhaps the best known of the King's mistresses. It is by Boucher (1703—1770) and includes one of her Papillons, named Inez.

In the 17th century the Papillon had reached Spain, and it is here that we find our first evidence of the erect-eared variety. This is in the Velasquez (1598—1660) portrait of Prince Phillip Prosper, which is in the Kunsthistorisches Museum in Vienna.

King Charles II, though already mentioned as an owner of an Italian Greyhound, is, of course, better known to dog-lovers for the spaniels named after him. There are many paintings in which both figure and one of especial interest, is that which is sometimes known as the Pineapple Picture. By Henry Danckerts (1630—1678) it shows the King with two of his spaniels being presented with the first pineapple grown in England (Sir Phillip Sassoon, Bt., Private Collection). The close resemblance between the dogs in this painting and the Cavalier of today is a feature of this work.

One of the many delightful paintings by Sir Joshua Reynolds (1723—1792) is that of the Marlborough Family, in the Collection of the Duke of Marlborough. In this there are two toy spaniels, one certainly a Cavalier, and the other which might be either a Papillon or a Cavalier. In the centre

(1)

foreground of this picture there is also an example of an Italian Greyhound.

The Pug is another breed which has existed relatively unchanged for centuries. In the painting by Jacopo da Empoli (1554—1640) of a dwarf with Louis XIII's dogs there is a probable ancestor of the present day Pug. It also, incidentally, includes toy spaniels of that era, as well as other breeds mentioned later. One Pug is distinguished by having a portrait painted of himself alone. By Carl Gustav Pilo, and dated 1749, the painting is entitled The Ramels Family's Pug, and is in the National Museum, Stockholm. In fact there are a number of paintings in Swedish collections in which Pugs figure. One of more than usual interest is by David Ehrenstrahl, dated 1670, of Queen Hedvig Eleanora's dogs, including two Pugs, and one

Colour
'Fidelitas' by Ehrenstrahl,
(National Museum, Stockholm).
She is seen with an Italian
Greyhound.

59

(MALTESE DOG)

(LION DOG)

60

of her Papillons. This is in Gripsholm, Sweden, as is another, by an unknown artist, of an allegorical painting with two Pugs optimistically chasing a deer.

A few remarks should be made about the Maltese, known earlier as the Maltese Terrier. These elegant, snow-white dogs have been very much refined in recent years, and few early pictures can be positively identified with the Maltese of today. However, the small dog in the arms of the Dwarf in the Empoli painting mentioned earlier could well be a Maltese. So also could the dog in Adam and Eve in Eden, a joint work of Peter Paul Rubens (1577—1640) and Jan Bruegel (1520—1569), in the Maritshuis, The Hague. Others which feature similar dogs, include The Poor Man Lazarus and the Rich Man Epulone by Gabriel Metsu (1615—1690) and Vanity, by Hans Memling (1430—1495), which also includes an Italian Greyhound, these are both in the Strasbourg Gallery.

Finally should be mentioned, briefly, a toy breed of some rarity, and of which very few are known to be in England. This is the Little Lion Dog, which is unique amongst the toy breeds in that it is clipped in a Lion cut similar to that of the Poodle. In fact, Lion Dog breeders have been known to claim that Poodles copied this cut from the Little Lions. The Central figure in the Empoli picture would seem to date the Little Lion Dog as being established on the European mainland in the 16th or early 17th century, but it is thought to have originated in the Mediterranean Islands earlier. It had penetrated to France well back in the past, seemingly, from evidence of a sculpture on a tomb in Amiens Cathedral. A painting in private hands in Spain, by Goya, of the Duchess of Alba, shows that the breed existed in that country in the late 18th or early 19th century.

In this Chapter, we have touched but the fringe of the vast resources of the art world in which toy dogs can be identified. Though mention has been made by name of a number of famous artists of the past, many, many more could have been instanced. It is almost impossible to find an art collection of any consequence in which there is not one or more paintings or sculptures in which one or other of these breeds figures.

A Maltese dog and a Little Lion Dog.

Possibly the most complete and painstaking representation of dogs in classical art. Roman sculptures of the 1st century AD.

5 RACING DOGS

The sport of coursing is one of the oldest in the world. This type of hunting, where the quarry is followed by sight and not scent, probably first took place in the Middle East. The hounds used there four thousand years ago are recognizably the same type as the Greyhound and Saluki of today. These are dogs built for speed. Their method of hunting is to view their quarry and overtake it within a comparatively short distance, rather than follow a scent and wear down their victim with persistent pursuit. Not only are they the fastest dogs, they are also those with the keenest sight. In the clear desert air, Salukis are credited with watching the flight of birds over half a mile away.

The group of breeds that were used for coursing, and latterly for racing, are known variously as Gazehounds, Sight-hounds or Windhounds. The best known is the Greyhound. The Arabs used them for coursing gazelles and the Ancient Greeks for coursing hares. They are still used for coursing hares in Britain today, but are much more widely known as racing dogs. The Saluki was used in the Middle East for coursing gazelle. The Afghan Hound hunted deer and the smaller antelope in its native land. Arabian Greyhounds were taken to Russia in the seventeenth century and crossed with hardier Russian breeds to create the Borzoi, a dog used for hunting wolves. In Scotland the Deerhound appears to have been in existence for as long as we have written records. Built to tackle larger deer and travel across rougher country, the Deerhound is the largest and heaviest of the group. The smallest member of the Gazehounds is the Whippet, a comparatively modern breed created in the nineteenth century for racing, though they have also been used for both coursing and ratting.

Greyhounds rounding a corner at speed.

A Champion Greyhound at Cruft's Show

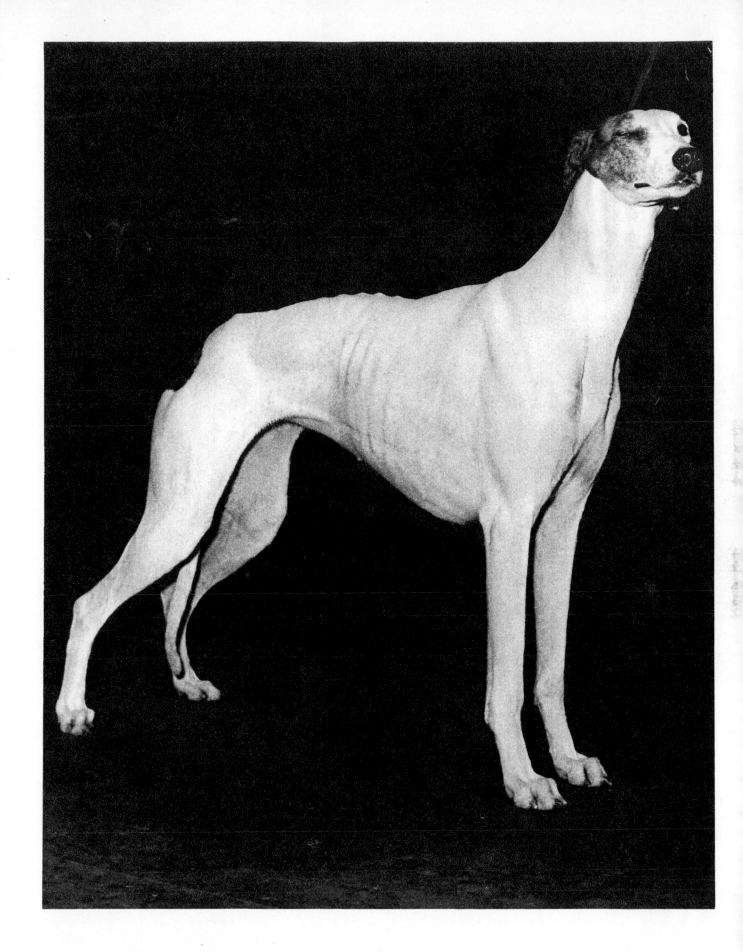

The winning Greyhound coming up to the post in a race at Wimbledon Stadium.

The speed of a running dog depends on the length and rapidity of the stride, and the gait used by these hounds is similar to that used by nature's fastest sprinters, the cheetah and some of the antelopes like the pronghorn. This can best be described as a series of extended leaps. The animal pushes off with the hindlegs and becomes fully extended in the air with the forelegs stretched out as far as possible in front. When the forelegs touch the ground the hindlegs are still in the air and are drawn forward under the body to land in their turn in front of the forelegs, ready for another propulsive effort. The whole is a jack-knife effect depending greatly on the back muscles, which expand and contract like a powerful spring.

When we consider the coursing breeds as a whole, it is obvious that they are all built on the same lines. They have long legs and well angulated

shoulders, allowing them to reach forward for maximum length of stride. They have long, flexible spines with muscular and slightly arched loins. They have plenty of heart and lung room, achieved, not by a broad chest which would prevent them galloping smoothly, but by the depth of the rib cage. They have comparatively wide hips and powerful hindquarters. The speed of a Greyhound possibly depends more on the muscular development of the thighs than any other single factor, and it is interesting that Greyhounds are born with a proportionately larger heart and larger pelvic muscle mass. These genetic advantages are further improved by training. The Afghan, one of the slower of this group, has wide-set, prominent hipbones. Built to travel across mountainous country, the Afghan excels in negotiating obstacles at speed and makes an excellent hurdler.

Whereas coursing was done for sport, dog racing has always depended on the interest of betting on the result for its financial support. The earliest racing was organized by miners in the North of England. Quite what was used to create those first racing dogs we don't know. Somewhere among their ancestry were the speedy terrier types which had been matched in the rat pits. A kind of park coursing was popular then, where bagged rabbits were freed in an enclosed space and dogs were matched to see which could kill the greater number out of a specified total. Fast dogs with plenty of stamina were needed for this and various greyhound/terrier crosses were used. From these motley beginnings Whippets or rag dogs emerged.

These early Whippet races were over two hundred yards, which a good dog would cover in twelve seconds or less. The handicapping was by weight, the heaviest dog was at the back and his lighter opponents gained a yard for every pound. From puppyhood the dogs were encouraged to worry a piece of cloth, until the sight of someone waving a rag was enough to produce a frenzy of excitement. After the weigh-in before a race, the Whippet was held by someone called a 'slipper', while the rag-man retreated up the track to the finishing line waving his cloth and shouting encouragement to the dog. At the starting pistol the dog, with its attention focused on the rag, was launched up the track by the slipper, whose skill ensured that the dog landed smoothly in full stride.

When a racing dog could earn more at a meeting than its owner could by a week's work, competition was naturally very keen. A good deal of chicanery went on and Whippet racing was never considered a respectable sport. A good slipper and rag-man gave a dog an advantage and the handicapping wasn't foolproof. Previous form wasn't a reliable guide as it was too easy to slow a dog deliberately, and 'ringing' i.e. substituting one dog for another, was not unknown. The best trainers however were very skilled in getting their dogs fit. The art of conditioning any racing dog is to get hard muscular condition without the animal carrying an extra ounce of flesh. This is achieved by a graded amount of exercise and a rigidly controlled diet. The

An Afghan Hound clearing a hurdle at tremendous speed in a race at a stadium in Munich, Germany.

Two Whippets set off at speed after the dummy hare at an amateur, 'no betting, no bookies' meeting in the north of England.

Greyhounds racing away from the trap at an amateur meeting in Germany.

Whippets were muzzled most of the time to prevent them scavenging, and were fed only on the best, regardless of what their owners could afford.

Old-style Whippet racing died out in the 1920s, helped in its decline by the popularity of Greyhound racing, where the controls were tight enough to prevent the more obvious trickeries. There is a revival of this sport which began in the 1950s, triggered off by show enthusiasts who wanted to see if their dogs could still race. Handicapping is now on form, and the dogs have to start with all four feet on the ground.

This photograph af an amateur race in which less-experienced Whippets are partaking, shows how ground is lost at the start. It is a fair bet that the first dog away from the trap will be first or second in the race.

This revival of amateur racing has received fresh impetus from the continent where the Union Internationale Clubs de Levriers organizes races for all the coursing breeds. There are fourteen amateur tracks in Holland and about the same number in Germany. These tracks are modelled on the best Greyhound tracks with the same sort of banking, starting boxes and the lure of a mechanical hare. At championship events hounds from up to six different countries will be competing.

Each breed runs separate races, and, in the numerically stronger breeds, the sexes are also divided. Middle distance races are favoured, with Whippets doing 350 metres and the larger breeds 475 metres. Approximate comparative times suggest that Afghans are the slowest, travelling at 28—29 m.p.h. Borzois are about a mile per hour faster, and Salukis faster still by the same amount. The real speed merchants are the Whippets who are travelling at 33—34 m.p.h. and the Greyhounds doing 35—36 m.p.h. The speed record for the fastest Greyhound on a professional track is constantly being broken but stands currently at 38.67 m.p.h.

To most people the phrase 'dog racing' means only one thing, professional Greyhound racing. This takes place not only in Great Britain and the United States but also in Australia and Spain. Though the rules and regulations differ slightly from country to country, in each the sport is controlled by a single authoritative body, whose inspectors or stewards rigidly enforce the rules. This ensures a fairer return for the punter and helps explain the

Six Afghan hounds breaking the trap in an experiment to see whether they can race the Greyhound. Although they were all off to a good start their interest soon waned, and one even gave up altogether.

The Off'. Two Whippets neck and neck as they break the trap.

Previous page
A large crowd watching Greyhounds coming round the final bend of the race. In the bottom right hand corner of the picture the dummy hare can be seen.

continued attraction of 'going to the dogs'.

Greyhound racing developed naturally from coursing, and all dogs racing in Britain have to be registered with the National Coursing Club before being accepted for registration by the National Greyhound Racing Club. In 1876, artificial coursing was tried as a sporting novelty in London. The Greyhounds chased a mechanical hare which was propelled by a windlass along a straight track. The idea did not catch on but was revived in America in the 1900s with an oval track and an electrically controlled hare. Again interest was meagre until absenteeism at afternoon meetings prompted the promoters to stage evening meetings where floodlighting immediately added the drama that pulled in the crowds. Florida was the state where the boom

first got under way and it still has more tracks than any other. Each state has its own State Racing Commission which operates a system of supervision through independent stewards. Races have eight or nine runners and the track surface is usually a sand and loam one. All dogs are graded according to previous form in an easily comprehensible system.

Though regulations vary between countries, the aims of racing are the same everywhere, and the British system illustrates the kind of control considered necessary. Where enormous sums are gambled on a sport, constant vigilance is needed to prevent fraudulent practices. Whippet racing declined in Britain partly because it got the reputation for being crooked and every effort has always been made by the National Greyhound Racing

'The Sport of Queens' — Greyhound racing — is a big winter attraction in Florida.

(1) A muzzled Greyhound waiting for the race.

(2) *Colour*
A Greyhound race in America.

(3) A Saluki

(4) Two Afghan Hounds

(5) Junia — the world's highest paid dog.

Club to make sure the same does not happen in Greyhound racing.

Any dog racing on a British track has to have registration papers from the National Coursing Club or the Irish Stud Book as well as from the National Greyhound Racing Club. These papers also include an identifying description, accurate and detailed enough to distinguish the animal without any possibility of mistake. Some countries insist on ear tattoos as well. Such a dog will be kennelled and trained by a licensed trainer attached to a particular dog track. On this home track, the more run-of-the-mill dogs will be raced in whichever grade of race the racing manager considers most suitable. Dogs which prove themselves top class will be trained and entered for Open races, which as the name implies, are not confined to entries from the track's kennels. A number of private trainers are also licenced by the N.G.R.C., but such licences are not granted lightly.

A young greyhound, called appropriately enough a 'sapling', will be put into training when it is about fifteen months old. The dog's desire to chase a mechanical hare is often kindled by allowing it to course a live one. Obviously too, the animal must be accustomed to wearing racing colours and the obligatory cage muzzle. A natural aversion to the starting traps has to be overcome and all the while the dog's muscular condition has to be built up until it reaches the peak of physical fitness. As each dog has individual needs, the trainer's art consists of adjusting food and exercise requirements to get the best from each animal. Greyhounds can be as temperamental as any other star performer, and maintaining a fine edge on the dog's enthusiasm for racing, is one of the hallmarks of a good trainer.

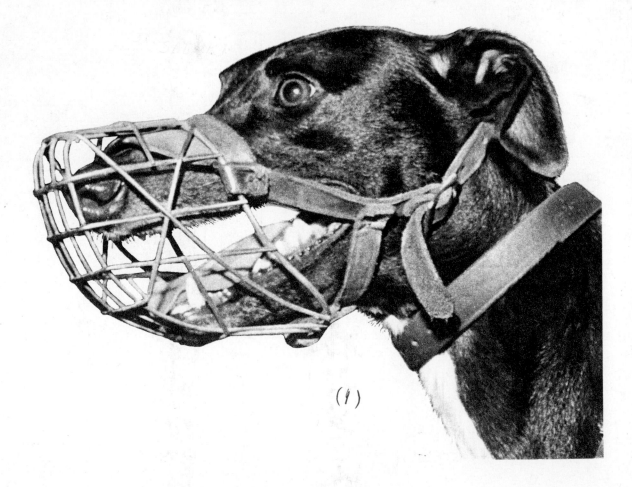

(1)

(3) SALUKI

(4) AFGHAN HOUNDS

DOGS OF FILM AND TELEVISION

6

For a long time dogs have been trained as entertainers. Circus and music hall acts featuring dogs have been popular all over the world for as long as the circus and the music hall have been in existence. Dogs have had parts in stage plays too but never to any great extent, and it is interesting to note that only one dog appears in any Shakespeare play — the dog 'Crab' in 'The Two Gentlemen of Verona'.

Not surprisingly, dogs proved successful film actors right from the start of silent movies. The name Rin Tin Tin was at one time as well known as that of any human star and even today there are television series with a dog of that name. Not the same dog of course, as the original Rin Tin Tin died in 1932.

A great boom in canine film stars was started by the famous collie Lassie. Soon after the outstanding success of M.G.M.'s film 'Lassie Come Home' it was estimated that Hollywood had some 250 professionally trained dogs working in its studios. This demand for dogs enabled trainers to form their own trade union, the Animal Owners and Handlers Association Inc., which looked after the interests of animals and their handlers, and did much to raise their working standards.

Such a state of affairs has not yet been reached in Britain but nevertheless there are professional trainers who specialize in training animals for film and television work. These include myself, and the reason why I refer to my

Colour
Two scenes from 'The Forsyte Saga' of Balthazar with Jolly and Holly, and of Ting-a-ling, the Pekinese, in Fleur's arms.

James Brown with Rin Tin Tin. Not the original Rin Tin Tin, which died in 1932, but one of his several successors.

79

Dubsky's Football Dogs, during their act in Bertram Mills Circus at Olympia, London.

own dogs more than to others is simply because I know more about them.

Dogs used in a circus or music hall act are very different from those used in film and television work. In the circus ring or on stage the dogs appear before your very eyes. You can see not only what the dogs do, but also what the handler does right there and then. But on the cinema or television screen you only see what the dog appears to have done. You cannot see the handler or know what he is doing. Indeed you are not supposed to know that there is a handler there, for he is hidden at all times from the camera's view; and if the dog works well you will have no idea where he or she is.

In an act a dog (or troupe of dogs) works to a routine. One trick follows another in strict rotation day after day. But in the studio there is no such

routine and a dog may well have to carry out some action hatched in the director's brain only five minutes earlier. Unlike his circus friend who only does what a dog can do, the film dog has often to appear almost human and do things which no sensible dog would dream of doing! Perhaps the biggest difference arises from the fact that the film dog nearly always 'belongs' to an artist and should give the impression that he really is the artist's own dog, which is no easy feat if they only met a couple of hours earlier.

Few people have seen the inside of a film or television studio and therefore can have little idea of the qualities which go to make a canine film star. Contrary to common belief intelligence is not the first essential. Indeed intelligence can be a big handicap and indeed several directors who have asked for an intelligent dog then expect it to do the stupidest things! The

Virginia McKenna (left) and Jennifer Jones, holding her dog Flush in a scene from 'The Barretts of Wimpole Street'.

Gwen Watford as Elizabeth Barrett holding the same Flush in the BBC's version of 'The Barrets of Wimpole Street'.

Flush acted in another film 'The Snorkel' and is here seen with Mandy Miller, the child actress, who was one of the stars of the film.

first essential is a bold, friendly nature. The dog must not be worried by any sort of distraction and must be friendly with anyone who is friendly towards him. And if he is not too friendly by nature then it is a great help if he is always greedy for food!

Flush who played Elizabeth Barrett's dog in M.G.M.'s 'The Barretts of Wimpole Street' never really liked Jennifer Jones. But she was so greedy that she would always go to her in anticipation of the biscuits which she invariably carried. She was always given one on the rehearsals, as a result of which she would go back to look for another on the 'take'. This was not possible when she appeared in the B.B.C.'s version of the same play, as it was transmitted live. Fortunately she took to Gwen Watford right away and snuggled up to her quite naturally — as she would to anyone she liked. In 'The Snorkel' she and Mandy Miller became very friendly and there were no problems at all.

Incidentally Flush was supposed to be a male in 'The Barretts of Wimpole Street'. She was also a very intelligent dog which did have its drawbacks. She would rush and scratch at a door to try to open it. But if it did not open she would simply run round the end of the 'flat' in which all studio doors are fixed. A stupid dog would never think of doing that — certainly not as quickly as Flush.

For big film parts dogs nearly always have a double and a stand-in. The double is a dog similar to the star which can take over if necessary. In America it is quite usual to use several doubles, each good at different things, and to change them according to the action. In Britain there is insufficient work for anyone to keep so many dogs and we have therefore to teach one dog to carry out more different actions. However, I am pleased to say that many American directors and producers with whom I have worked are very complimentary about British trained dogs. But they are more insistent on having at least one double in case the star turns ill, goes lame or is in any other way put out of action. When there is a lot of work for the dog in a film a double can be a great help in doing some of the less important scenes, thus keeping the star fresh and keen for the more important parts.

So far as dogs are concerned a stand-in is usually a dummy dog or just a cushion of similar size and colour. It is simply there to enable the lighting cameraman to light the set. This may take several hours and gives rise to the accounts you may have heard from amateurs as to how they and their dog had to stay under hot lights for ages and ages. This is very unkind, quite unnecessary and rarely happens with professional handlers, for the dog should also be given a star's consideration.

Most film dogs are taught to stand, sit or lie down in response to either a hand signal or word of command, and to stay in any position in which they are placed. They are also taught to come when called, either quickly or slowly, and to go from one person to another on a command given either by the person from whom they are going or the one to whom they are coming. Picking up any object on command and holding it is another useful exercise, also barking on command, which is very easy to teach some dogs but practically impossible to teach others. It should be remembered that the dog must carry out the action to split second timing, and not just when it feels like doing it. After the basic exercises we teach individual dogs to do the things they are best suited for — and most likely to be asked to do. For instance sheepdogs are taught to work sheep and Alsatians to do criminal work. If the script calls for some special action, a dog may have to be specially taught to do it. This is another difference between film and circus trainer. The latter having taught a dog a particular trick can expect to go on using it for years probably for the dog's working life. But a film trainer may spend weeks or months teaching a dog something which it will only need to do once, or at the most a few times.

In her first film my Pekinese Mandy had, amongst other things, to rush in and out through a pussy flap in a door. This was made specially for her so that it could be pushed open from either side, and she took to it with tremendous enthusiasm, banging the flap with her flat face. So much so that the first time she did it in the studio one electrician was heard exclaiming to his mate, 'Cor! Did you see that flippin' dog? It went straight through that door'. But in spite of all the time spent in teaching her and her ability in doing it Mandy has never been asked to go through a pussy flap again. In her

Mandy, a Pekinese, being held by Ingrid Bergman in 'The Yellow Rolls Royce'.

Marcello Mastroianni holding
Mandy in the film 'Diamonds for
Breakfast'.

latest film 'Diamonds for Breakfast' we taught her to pull a model Russian Troika and she was just as enthusiastic about that. But I doubt if there will ever be another script calling for a Pekinese pulling a cart!

Mandy's greatest asset as a film star is her tremendous courage and complete lack of fear. In 'The Yellow Rolls Royce' (in which her father was her double) Ingrid Bergman and Mandy are sitting in a hotel which is bombed. This was done in the studio where the confined atmosphere makes any explosion sound much worse than outside. This worried me a lot and the director, the late Anthony Asquith, asked the special effects boys to make some small bangs to see how Mandy would react. She just didn't react at all. In the actual scene the whole ceiling falls down while Ingrid Bergman and her darling 'Duchess' are supposed to cower in terror under the table. Ingrid Bergman looked terrified and probably was — but Mandy remained quite unconcerned. In 'Diamonds for Breakfast' the script calls for the dog to appear on a narrow ledge on the fifth floor of a London hotel. The director, Christopher Morohan, said that if I thought she would be afraid or there was any danger of her falling he would not insist on trying it — *but* he would very much like her to do it if possible. So I made a safety harness with nylon of 200 lb. breaking strain (Mandy weighs ten pounds) and placed her gently out of a window on to the ledge below. While I and everyone else held their breath she just sat there surveying all the people in the forecourt below with unconcerned interest.

While dogs are still being used as much as ever in feature films, those

which are best known to the general public are the ones they see on television. We have found that our best known dogs are invariably those appearing on a commercial currently appearing on the screen. But as soon as another dog appears the first one is soon forgotten.

Actually far more dogs appear in parts in television plays and series than in commercials. In many cases the parts are very small, often designed merely to provide a homely atmosphere. Because of this few people have any idea of the problems involved and many have said to me, 'But he didn't do anything did he?' I have trained and used dogs for many purposes and have found that the most difficult thing to get a dog to do, is to appear to be doing nothing quite naturally as if he were in his own home, but in fact, under the most unnatural conditions imaginable. On the film set it is not always possible to speak to the dog while the camera is running, but one can speak to him until the director says 'Action' and again as soon as he says 'Cut'. In the television studios, however, the cameras move from one scene to another and no one ever speaks above a whisper (except those taking part) and there is even a notice on the door asking, 'Are you wearing soft-soled shoes?' Artists are always more tensed up in television studios than before a film camera and everything builds up to the most unnatural atmosphere you could imagine. If a dog is to appear natural and relaxed under such conditions it must have complete confidence in its handler. And it will only do that if the handler has complete confidence in himself. Many dogs which appear tensed up and in a panic on the screen are merely reacting to a handler

Diana Rigg, alias Mrs Emma Peel, sitting holding two beautiful Borzois which took part in an episode in 'The Avengers'.

Sergeant Cluff (Leslie Sands) and
Clive, his faithful dog, in an
episode from the series 'Cluff'.

A close-up profile of Clive,
a pedigree Border Collie.

who is somewhere behind the cameras in an even worse state of nerves.

People who say, 'My dog could easily do that' are often right but whether he would do it to the exact split second timing called for in television is quite a different matter. With the small screen there is no point in having a dog somewhere around — he must be on his mark at the exact instant to co-ordinate with the dialogue and/or action of an artist or artists. If Sgt. Cluff and his faithful Clive came into the police station together the dog had to be exactly the same distance ahead or behind, as had been found right on rehearsal. Otherwise you might only see its tail at the bottom of the screen.

Clive is in real life a pedigree Border Collie bitch called Tuck and probably one of the best remembered dogs ever to appear in any series. This was undoubtedly due to the fact that she always looked conpletely at home and gave the impression that she really did belong to Cluff. In fact many people refused to believe that she did not belong to actor Leslie Sands and he received far more fan mail about her than I did. But he is the first to emphasize that no actor could control a dog and act at the same time. Supposing an actor is sitting in a chair asleep and the dog has to react to the approach of a stranger outside — how could he possibly tell it to bark at the door?

Like many of the best working dogs Tuck came to us as a problem dog. She was then three and a half years old and had developed some rather obnoxious habits such as chasing motor bikes (and tipping them over), fighting other bitches and nipping strangers. But the tremendous instinct to work and the desire to do something which leads to trouble in so many pet dogs also provides the essential raw material on which trainers can work. Given the opportunity to do something positive Tuck became an excellent sheepdog and one of the most versatile film dogs we have ever owned. In the film 'Postman's Knock' she rushes right along a platform at Marylebone station, through crowds of people, picks out Spike Milligan, and snatches a bundle of letters he is carrying in his hand. In 'Casino Royale' she selects one man from a crowd of about forty, all fighting in a pub brawl; seizes

him by the seat and hangs on while he spins round and round on top of a table. And she did that when she was eleven years old.

The nondescript mongrel who plays the part of Balthazar in the B.B.C. version of' The Forsyte Saga' is Garry, a pedigree Bearded Collie, but not a very good show specimen. Most of the exterior scenes in TV plays are filmed, and when there is no dialogue one can usually speak to the dog. But in the scene where Balthazar dies it was necessary, for technical reasons, to record the sound of his feet rustling the leaves as he creeps through the bushes. I was amused to read Kenneth More's report of this scene in a women's magazine. We had, he said, specially trained the dog to lie down and die in response to a whistle which sounded like a bird in the background! A fascinating idea but highly improbable when one considers that it was only when we took the dog before the camera that we were told the sound would be running.

In the same serial is a little dog called Skipper which befriends Nora Nicholson, one of the Forsyte aunts. This name was chosen because our

little crossbred Papillon/Cavalier Kings Charles Spaniel, called Skipper was booked for the part. But when I was up in London with him for the camera rehearsal he slipped a disc playing with another dog. This caused quite some consternation at the B.B.C. which, unlike American film producers, does not pay to have a double standing by. However, my wife came up with three substitutes from which was chosen 'Duffy' a wonderful little shaggy dog, a cross between a Yorkshire Terrier and a Shih Tzu. But there was no time to change the credit cards and as the cast had been referring to the dog as Skipper during rehearsal that is what he was called.

We had previously had a big part for a cat in a play with Nora Nicholson. She is a charming old lady who adores cats and likes dogs too, but unfortunately cannot stand having her face licked by a dog. Duffy on the other hand just could not understand why anyone should resent being licked by him and became quite worried about it. For this reason his performance in 'The Forsyte Saga' is not as natural as in some other parts he has had.

People often say to me, 'I don't think it is right using animals on films

The 'Blue Peter' animals,
Petra and Jason.

Edison, one of the stars of 'Chitty
Chitty Bang Bang' with a cigarette.

Richard Attenborough taking
a kick at the Basset in 'The Bliss
of Mrs. Blossom'.

Mandy with Eric Sykes, Terry
Thomas and a Great Dane in
'Kill or Cure'.

and television — my dog would hate it'. The answer to that is that their dog
would be quite useless. One does see dogs on the screen absolutely loathing
every minute of it. These are usually nervous dogs, belonging to amateurs.
It is really wicked to take a nervous dog into a studio, but no worse than
taking it shopping in a busy thoroughfare. Professionals can only earn
a living by keeping bold dogs with initiative — extroverts, show-offs or
whatever you like to call them. This type of dog simply loves working in
a studio or anywhere else and loathes sitting at home doing nothing.

7 HEROIC DOGS

What's the use of a dog? We know they make good companions, they are nice to take for walks, and even make good foot warmers! But what can they do which is of *real* benefit to man?

The answer is that they do much, much more than many people could believe is possible. For example, dogs have played their part in battle for centuries. In the Middle Ages, dogs took to war wearing complete sets of miniature armour. As time has gone on 'fighting' dogs have disappeared, but during the First World War they took on more highly beneficial and very dangerous work.

Thousands of privately owned dogs 'joined up', and these well trained dogs were responsible for running messages across dangerous territories, frequently between two men whom they loved and trusted, at the same time carrying some very welcome hot soup! Patrol work and guard duty became less of a gamble with the help of a dog's sharp eyes, hearing and sense of

The story of the dog Gelert at Beddgelert in North Wales.

GELERT'S GRAVE

IN THE 13TH CENTURY, LLEWELYN, PRINCE OF NORTH WALES, HAD A PALACE AT BEDDGELERT. ONE DAY HE WENT HUNTING WITHOUT GELERT "THE FAITHFULL HOUND" WHO WAS UNACCOUNTABLY ABSENT. ON LLEWELYN'S RETURN, THE TRUANT STAINED AND SMEARED WITH BLOOD, JOYFULLY SPRANG TO MEET HIS MASTER. THE PRINCE ALARMED HASTENED TO FIND HIS SON, AND SAW THE INFANT'S COT EMPTY, THE BEDCLOTHES AND FLOOR COVERED WITH BLOOD. THE FRANTIC FATHER PLUNGED HIS SWORD INTO THE HOUND'S SIDE THINKING IT HAD KILLED HIS HEIR. THE DOG'S DYING YELL WAS ANSWERED BY A CHILD'S CRY. LLEWELYN SEARCHED AND DISCOVERED HIS BOY UNHARMED. BUT NEAR BY LAY THE BODY OF A MIGHTY WOLF WHICH GELERT HAD SLAIN, THE PRINCE FILLED WITH REMORSE IS SAID NEVER TO HAVE SMILED AGAIN HE BURIED GELERT HERE THE SPOT IS CALLED

BEDDGELERT

A message dog used in the trenches in the First World War in France.

A dog used as an ammunition carrier in the Second World War in France. The soldier is taking from the dog some drums of ammunition.

smell. During the Second World War, dogs were even trained to detect
mines!

Such a dog was Ricky, a young Welsh Sheepdog, who had been bombed
out of his home. Luckily a family from Bromley, Kent gave him a home and
then, as he was found to have an extremely keen sense of smell, he joined the
Royal Army Veterinary Corps and landed in Europe on D-Day. Ricky worked
hard and fearlessly throughout Europe, locating hidden and buried mines,
and indicating where they were by sitting beside them.

On December 3rd, 1944, Ricky was working along the verges of a canal

Colour
Huskies pulling a sledge.

Fawn Cairn Terrier

Labrador *next page*

Police handlers with their Alsatians

bank at Nederweert in Holland when a mine exploded. The Section Commander was badly injured and Ricky was wounded in the head. Many dogs
would have panicked and run, frantic with fear, through the mine-infested
fields — but Ricky was no ordinary dog! The Sergeant needed medical
attention as quickly as possible and yet nobody dared approach him in case
they should detonate a mine. Ricky sniffed quietly around, walking first this
way and then another. The soldiers watched intently as the clever little dog
showed them the path — the way to reach the wounded man and carry him
to safety. When Ricky returned to England, his head wound had healed but

CAIRN TERRIER

LABRADOR

ALSATIANS

(1)

he still had a nasty scar on his head to tell the tale, and the P.D.S.A presented him with their Dickin Medal.

The Dickin Medal, or Animal's V.C., was named after Mrs. M. E. Dickin, C.B.E., the founder of the P.D.S.A. It was only awarded during war time, and altogether eighteen dogs have received the medal. The P.D.S.A. are fully aware that their medals and awards don't benefit the dog in any way. Their purpose is simply to impress upon the public the important work which animals are capable of doing.

Antis, an Alsation, also won the medal. He stayed with his master, who was a Czech airman, all through the war, even when he made a daring escape. Rob made over twenty parachute jumps when serving for the special air unit responsible for finding wounded men in desolate places. Judy, a pedigree

Colour
Police Alsatian being trained to (1) attack.

A Royal Army Veterinary Corps Sergeant prods for concealed mines, (2) which his dog has guided him to.

Tudor, a Labrador Retriever, is the Army's first dog parachutist. (3) He is here being trained to jump from an aircraft into areas where casualties may be lying.

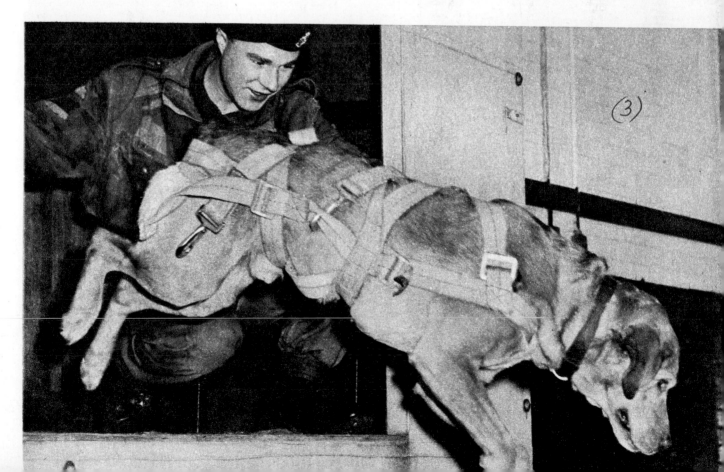

Beauty and other members of the P.D.S.A. rescue squad at work (1) during the Second World War.

During the Second World War the Ministry of Aircraft (2) Production trained dogs to locate persons trapped under collapsed buildings.

Beauty digging through the debris, after a bomb has fallen, (3) to find any bodies lying underneath.

Pointer, was not only a Dickin medallist, she was the only dog ever officially registered as a Prisoner of War. She spent two years in captivity in the East, boosting the men's morale and undoubtedly saving lives by warning of approaching snakes, scorpions and other dangerous animals.

Another group of these war time heroes worked in the cities. These were the dogs that were specially trained to find people buried under bombed buildings. Many people managed to survive the actual bombing, only to be threatened with death by being trapped under the debris. These people were more than grateful when they heard the sound of a rescue dog digging.

The trainers and handlers of these dogs were amazed to notice the apparent dedication with which they worked. One particular Dickin medallist, an Alsatian called Una, would indicate whether the trapped victim was still alive or not. If the victim was still breathing, she dug frantically, if the victim was already dead, she would quietly sit down and wait.

Beauty used to accompany her master to the scene of air-raids. He was a P.D.S.A. official and so, of course, he was particularly interested in the

②

③

bombed animals' welfare. Beauty soon learnt to sniff out and dig out trapped dogs. In fact she was responsible for digging out · no less than 63 dogs. Sometimes she would dig so hard that her paws would bleed and so the P.D.S.A. fitted her with two pairs of leather boots.

But not all heroic animals were war time dogs by any means. Sandor Gubonyi, a Hungarian, was driving his truck through the wildest and most desolate part of the West Queensland outback. The truck went into a rut, Sandor was thrown out and the truck rolled on top of him. His back was badly injured and he was all alone — apart from a brown and white cattle dog called Bimbo. It was January, and the hot Australian sun was beating relentlessly down upon the poor man. Suddenly, a flock of predatory crows appeared, and swooped down upon him. Sandor buried his head in his arms and waited for the sharp beaks to seek out his eyes and uncovered flesh — but another noise joined the loud crowing. Bimbo was leaping up at the enormous birds, barking and snapping each time they dived. Eventually Sandor was rescued and he certainly had a lot to thank his dog for.

In Austria, heroic actions by dogs are almost an every day occurrence. The magnificent Austrian Mountain Rescue Service has been responsible for finding thousands of men and women trapped by the terrible 'White Death', the avalanches of the snow-covered Tyrol. The Alsatians and the Belgian Sheepdogs have been trained to such a high degree that they can find men and women, even when they are buried beneath several feet of snow and ice.

There have been many great heroes in the Austrian Rescue Team. Lupo,

St. Bernard dogs with the monks of the St. Bernard Hospice. The breed was named after Bernard de Menthon six centuries ago, and is famous for rescuing lost wayfarers in the Swiss Alps.

This Alsatian is used by the Austrian Mountain Rescue Team to locate unfortunate victims of avalanches.

Previous page
Eskimos with their Huskies in Greenland.

Rudi, the little Dachshund who rescued his master's friend from being battered by a bull in Scotland. (1)

Laddie, the Golden Retriever, who pulled a water-logged boat full of children to dry land. (2)

A Great Dane called Juliana who tackled an incendiary bomb on her master's premises during an air raid in Bristol in the Second World War. (3)

Monty, an Alsatian, who ran three miles to the son of Mrs. Taylor in Melbourne, when she collapsed with a heart attack and could not reach the telephone. (4)

an Alsatian, worked tirelessly for ten years. Mira, Zorn and Pia were three of the heroic workers in the terrible winter of 1951. These dogs work with such devotion that even when their eyes ache from the sun or the snow, even when their breathing becomes difficult at the high altitudes and their thick coats freeze with ice, they are still able to work and save another life.

Of course, these dogs are trained to do their work, but many go far beyond their training. Even pet dogs can achieve the ranks of greatness. Rudiger von Stoer from Renfrewshire, Scotland was one of these. He was a little Dachshund. Rudi, as he was usually called, had been taken on a trip to a farm by his master Commander Mowat, and a friend, Mr. Hugh Welch. Suddenly an enormous bull charged at Mr. Welch and threw him to the ground. Luckily, Mr. Welch was a strong man and he held on to the horns and tried to push the beast away, but the bull's great head only pushed further down until it was rammed on to his chest.

Commander Mowat was some distance away but he ran to help. Suddenly, a short-legged hound was there first. Without hesitation, Rudi flung himself at the bull until it was forced to leave its prisoner and deal with the annoying little dog which was snapping round its ankles. Lowering its head, it caught Rudi on its horns, goring him badly. But still Rudi kept on, until the huge beast gave a snort of disgust — and ran away!

Laddie was a magnificent Golden Retriever owned by Mr. Player of Fishbourne, Isle of Wight. One day in 1947, Mr. Player's grandson and

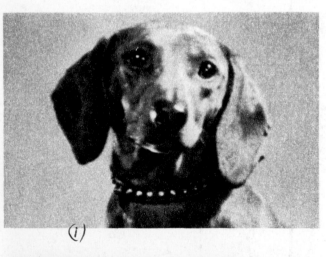

(1)

(2)

(3)

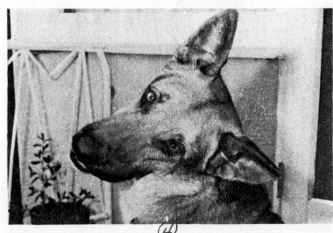

(4)

a friend, decided to take out a rowing boat. They had not gone far before the current began to carry them out to sea, and the boat filled with water.

Laddie had been playing happily on the beach. Suddenly, he heard a cry, turned and looked out to sea. Diving in, he swam strongly towards the boat. The boys saw him coming — but what could a dog do? The brave dog pushed his strong body against the side of the boat and one of the boys leant over and grabbed his collar. But instead of getting into the boat, Laddie struck off for the beach — pulling the boat behind him! When the boys got back, they told everyone about Laddie and, in February 1948, the Mayor of Fishbourne presented him with a medal.

The R.S.P.C.A. also present awards to families owning dogs which have shown 'bravery' in some way. One of their more recent awards was presented to a young mongrel called Wendy.

Wendy was twelve months old when the R.S.P.C.A. found her a good home with the Bolding family of Weymouth, Dorset. Nine-year-old Nigel Bolding used to take Wendy for walks and one day in February, 1966, they were exploring the heathland at Bowleaze Cove when Nigel slipped down a steep bank into a bog.

Wendy was terrified. She was rather a nervous little dog, afraid of anything strange, but obviously something had to be done. For a while, she just barked, but then she turned quickly and ran away, and Nigel felt sure she had run away in panic. But the little dog had different ideas.

Wendy, a nervous little dog, who ran all the way home to inform her mistress that her son Nigel Bolding had slipped down a steep bank into a bog in Dorset.

Nigel Bolding holding the Dickin Medal which was awarded to Wendy for getting rescue to him.

The R.S.P.C.A. plaque which was awarded to Major, an Alsatian, for rescuing two lives. While walking along the Thames bank at Hammersmith, his master saw a child in difficulties in the river. He jumped in, but was soon himself in difficulties. Major came to the rescue, and his master clung to him with one hand while catching the child with the other, and all managed to get ashore.

Back at the Boldings' house, Mrs. Bolding was amazed to see a very muddy and bedraggled Wendy running up the front path. She felt sure Nigel couldn't be far away because Wendy was much too nervous to travel far on her own. But she was really surprised when she followed the little dog over a very busy road to a cove a mile and a half from home. There they found a man and a woman already pulling Nigel out of the bog. Wendy had helped in more ways than she had imagined as her barking had attracted them to the cove. The R.S.P.C.A. were very proud of Wendy because she had overcome her natural fears so bravely, and so they presented the Boldings with their special plaque.

Thane was an eleven month old retriever. In August 1966, Mr. and Mrs. Lomax of Bolton, Lancashire were taking Thane for a walk beside a lake at Southport. They stopped to watch a little Cairn Terrier retrieving a plastic dish from the lake as people threw it in for him. One throw was too far out for such a small dog, but it swam out — only to realize that it hadn't enough strength to swim back. Everyone watched in horror as the poor little thing floundered about — but Thane wasn't just watching, he was acting! As quick as lightening, he dived in, grabbed the terrier by the scruff of its neck and dragged it back to the shore where it was quickly revived. Thane had

The War in Vietnam. Shane, a Marine scout dog, picks up an enemy's scent during a patrol near Da Nang. The dog's handler was trained with Shane in the United States before coming to Vietnam, and it is the first time that the U. S. Marines have used scout dogs in combat since the Second World War.

Rusty, the Ministry of Aviation's air-crash dog 'detective'. The dog was trained to seek out vital clues after air-crashes which humans often cannot find.

The famous 'Greyfriars Bobby' in Edinburgh. In 1858 this faithful dog followed the remains of his master to Greyfriars Churchyard, and lingered near the grave until his death in 1872. This well and statue were erected in his memory.

A sad day for a blindman and his dog. Sally is now too old for the job and is becoming partly blind herself, so she must go into retirement after 13 years of faithful service.

achieved a new distinction by becoming the first dog to get a bravery award for rescuing another dog!

So . . . what is the use of a dog? Just ask the Bolding family, ask Sandor Gubonyi, Bimbo's master, and ask the thousands of men and women whose lives were saved on the battlefields, and under bombed sites. And ask the thankful people who were dug up alive from avalanches, not to mention those men and women whose active lives depend upon another unquestionable set of heroes — the Guide Dogs for the Blind.

On the P.D.S.A.'s Dickin Medal there are three simple words — 'We Also Serve'. And they most certainly do!

CARE OF DOGS 8

The dog has been Man's companion since time immemorial, a fact due principally to two basic characteristics, one of Man and one of the dog. Firstly, Man in his higher intellect has developed a compassion towards his fellow creatures to which the dog readily responds. Secondly, the domestic dog is so dependent in its nature upon its master that it flatters this compassion, providing a devoted friend at all times.

It follows, then, that if we are to create such a bond between ourselves and our dogs, we must realize all that this entails and accept the responsibility, for responsibility it is, of ensuring that the dog we befriend is provided with the way of life that its nature dictates. If we fail to do this, we must accept the consequences.

Dogs respond to the environment in which they live, and in order to establish a lasting, satisfying and fulfilling companionship with them, we must ensure that the environment we provide is the right one.

Both sides of a companionship must be content if it is to prove successful. The requirements of both parties should, therefore, be considered.

The requirements of the owner

1. FUNCTION — What we expect from our dog will have a considerable bearing on the facilities we should provide for it. Do we require simply a household pet or do we want a working dog?

2. HOME — What sort of home do we expect the dog to live in? Firstly, what size of dog do we think we can comfortably accommodate in our house and garden? Secondly, with what kind of home life must the dog be compatible? For instance, must it withstand the constant and sometimes provoking attentions of children, or must it be the kind that does not disturb old people?

3. COST — Dogs, if they are to be cared for properly, cost money. We must, therefore, be certain that the requirements of the dog we choose do not stretch our pockets too far. It is not only the cost of feeding that should be considered but also the cost of veterinary attention and kennelling.

4. RESILIENCE — What sort of life can we offer? Will the dog be required to travel a lot, to be left alone a lot, to go into kennels a lot, and so on?

The requirements of the dog

1. EXERCISE — No matter the size of the dog, it will require regular exercise. Furthermore, an energetic and lively dog appreciates more than a simple daily 'walk round the block'. We must, therefore, consider the facilities in our neighbourhood available for suitable exercise and decide how much time we are prepared regularly to devote to exercising our dog. *Never* resort to permitting the dog to exercise itself by roaming.

2. TRAINING — All dogs require to be trained properly if they are not to prove a constant source of embarrassment and frustration to their owners and annoyance to others. The essence of training is the establishment of what

Two Collies being put through their paces at the beginners' class of the St. Austell and District Canine Society's obedience training sessions. *(1)*

An English Setter and a Golden Retriever being taken for a walk during their training. *(2)*

Colour
Young puppy ———→ *(3)*

Portrait of Charles IV by Francisco Goya (Museum of Naples).

NEXT PAGE

Springer Spaniel and two Irish Setters. Both breeds make excellent gun dogs.

are known as 'conditioned responses'. What this means is that animals, which do not have the ability of reasoned thought, depend for all their controllable behaviour on the recognition of a standard set of circumstances or pattern of events. In simple terms, a house-trained dog does not go into the garden to urinate because it knows that it should not do such a thing in the house. On the contrary, house-training has established in it a 'conditioned response' which prevents it from going through the process of urination without the stimulus that is provided by its being out-of-doors. If this basic fact can be understood, it makes training much easier for both the owner and his dog. All training depends, therefore, on the repetition of the stimulus (the situation or the command) until the desired response becomes fully conditioned. To train a dog, then, all that is required is patience, kindness and understanding. If it does wrong, scold it; if it does right, praise it. *Never* employ physical punishment.

3. GROOMING — Every dog whether short-haired or long-haired, wiry or smooth, should be regularly groomed, not only to remove dead hairs and foreign objects from the coat but also to stimulate the production and secretion of the skin oils vital to a healthy coat. The only requirements are a strong comb, a stiff brush and about ten minutes each day. Furthermore, if the dog gets dirty, it should be bathed. A mild shampoo is ideal for this and afterwards the dog should be thoroughly dried before being allowed out-of-doors. Do not, however, bath the dog too often and never use a detergent.

4. FEEDING — The prime requirement for the health of a dog is, of course, that it receives a properly balanced diet. In addition to providing the correct quantities of the basic foods (proteins, carbohydrates and fats), it is also essential to ensure the intake of sufficient minerals and vitamins. There are many ways of meeting these nutritional requirements and the

(1)

(2)

(1)

ASSET HOUND
HETLAND SHEEPDOG

JACK RUSSELL TERRIER
CHESAPEAKE BAY RETRIEVER

BOXER
LAPPHOUND

CORGIS
BEAGLE

CHINESE CRESTED DOG ■

One of the hairless breeds which are believed to have originated in Africa, the Chinese Crested Dog has a tuft of long hair on the top of the skull and on the end of the tail. The skin colour is usually mottled.

CHOW CHOW ■ ● ▲

The Chow Chow was originally bred in China for its flesh and fur, which can be practically any solid colour. Usually distinguished by an abundant stand-off coat, there is also a smooth-coated variety.

CLUMBER SPANIEL ■ ● ▲

The Clumber is the most heavily built of the spaniels, weighing up to seventy pounds. Despite the beauty of its white, silky coat with the pale lemon markings on the head, the Clumber Spaniel has never been really popular.

Rusty   X

COCKER SPANIEL ■ ● ▲

The merry character and gentle disposition of the Cocker Spaniel led to it becoming the most popular breed in Britain during the 1940s. The variety of coat colours adds to the breed's attractions.

COLLIE ■ ● ▲

The Rough and the Smooth Collie are the same in conformation but the glory of the Rough's profuse coat, with its well-developed mane and frill, have made it by far the most popular of the two.

COONHOUND ●

There are number of American hound breeds developed especially for raccoon hunting but only the black-and-tan Coonhound is officially recognized by the American Kennel Club. Both Foxhound and Bloodhound were used to create it.

CURLY-COATED RETRIEVER ■ ● ▲

One of the rarest of the retrieving breeds, the Curly-coated Retriever is either black or liver. The tight, crisp curls of the coat contrast with the smooth hair on the head and muzzle.

DACHSHUND ■ ● ▲

These short-legged, long-bodied dogs were originally bred in Germany to bay badgers and hunt smaller game. There are three coat varieties, the smooth, the long-haired and the wire-haired, and in Britain the miniature varieties are recognized.

DALMATIAN ■ ● ▲

The sleek, white coat of the Dalmatian covered with its well-defined spots lent distinction to the fashionable carriages of the horse era. Now they are valued both for their appearance and their companionship.

DANDIE DINMONT TERRIER ■ ● ▲

The Dandie Dinmont is a tough little terrier with a crisp body coat and a soft silky top-knot. The melting expression of the eyes belies the independent character.

DEERHOUND ■ ● ▲

This ancient breed comes from the Highlands of Scotland where they were used for coursing deer. They are one of the few breeds where type has remained constant over the years.

DOBERMANN PINSCHER ■ ● ▲

The Dobermann takes its name from Louis Dobermann who created the breed as a guard dog *par excellence* in Germany in in the 1890s. The usual colour is black and tan and the breed is elegant, agile and fearless.

ELKHOUND ■ ● ▲

Called the Norwegian Elkhound in America, this Scandinavian breed has been known since Viking times. A powerful, compact, grey dog, the Elkhound excels in the tracking of game, as well as making a trustworthy, affectionate companion.

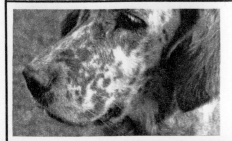

ENGLISH SETTER ■ ● ▲

The English Setter is thought by some to be one of the most beautiful of all dogs. The silky white coat can be freckled with black, lemon or liver and the conformation combines elegance with endurance.

ENGLISH SPRINGER ■ ● ▲
Springer Spaniels today are popular as gun dogs, being used to find and retrieve most kinds of game. They are usually liver and white in colour.

ENGLISH TOY TERRIER ■ ● ▲
Known as Toy Manchester Terriers in America, these diminutive animals are full of fire and courage. The glossy coat is black with rich mahogany markings.

FIELD SPANIEL ■ ●
The Field Spaniel resembles a longer-backed, more robustly built Cocker. The breed has been in existence for about a hundred years but is very low in numbers at the present time.

FINNISH SPITZ ■
The Finnish Spitz is a foxy looking animal with a reddish coat and a bushy tail curled tightly over the back. They were bred in Northern Scandinavia as bird dogs and watch-dogs.

FLAT-COATED RETRIEVER ■ ●
At the turn of the century the Flat-coated Retriever was one of the most popular of the gundogs. Though honest and reliable as workers, they are now rarely seen. The colour is usually black, occasionally liver.

FOXHOUND ■ ● ▲
The English Foxhound differs from the American in being slightly larger and more uniform in type. Nearly all Foxhounds are kept for sporting purposes only.

FOX TERRIER ■ ● ▲
Both the Smooth and Wire-haired Fox Terrier should have exactly the same conformation. Bred to run with the hounds and bolt foxes from their earths, they are gay, lively and game.

FRENCH BULLDOG ■ ● ▲

The French Bulldog is quite distinct from its English counter-part, being smaller and less exaggerated in shape. The colours can be brindle, fawn or pied. This breed has a great deal of charm and is very affectionate.

GERMAN SHEPHERD DOG ■ ● ▲

Known as the Alsatian in Britain, this breed can fairly claim to be the most popular in the world. Its discriminating intelligence has made it foremost in the working field and correspondingly well known as a family dog.

GERMAN SHORT-HAIRED POINTER ■ ●

Versatility as a gundog has made the German Short-haired Pointer well known in North America. The flat, coarse, white coat is heavily flecked and patched with liver.

GERMAN WIRE-HAIRED POINTER ■ ●

Though the most popular gundog in Germany, the Wire-haired Pointer is unknown in Britain, but it is well established in North America. The coat is wiry, water-repellent and completely weatherproof.

GLEN OF IMAAL TERRIER ■

This is a working terrier that is rarely seen in the show ring. As the Glen of Imaal Terrier was bred to tackle badgers, they are full of courage and tenacity.

GOLDEN RETRIEVER ■ ● ▲

The kindly nature of the Golden Retriever makes it very suitable as a family dog. The coat is slightly wavy and may be any shade from deep gold to cream.

GORDON SETTER ■ ● ▲

The black and tan Gordon Setter is the largest of the setters and tends to be a one man dog. They are steady reliable workers with a good deal of endurance.

GREAT DANE ■ ● ▲
The Great Dane is one of the largest breeds and combines power, elegance and symmetry. In the past they were used for hunting wild boar on the continent.

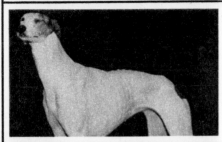

GREYHOUND ■ ● ▲
The Greyhound type is one of the most ancient of domestic dogs. Used for many centuries for coursing, most are now bred for the sport of Greyhound racing.

GRIFFON BRUXELLOIS ■ ● ▲
A toy dog of character, the Griffon's appeal owes much to its impudent expression. The wiry coat of the rough variety should include a distinct moustache and beard. The smooth variety is known as the Petit Brabançon.

GROENENDAEL ■ ● ▲
The Groenendael is the black variety of Belgian Sheepdog, and they are registered under the latter name in America. The coat is smooth, of medium length and with the suggestion of a ruff on the neck.

HARRIER ■ ● ▲
The Harrier is a hound intermediate in size between the Foxhound and the Beagle. Some are still used for hunting the hare but more are entered after foxes or used for drag hunting.

HUSKY ■ ● ▲
The Husky in Britain is a descendant of the sledge dogs used in Greenland. America has the Siberian Husky, a dog very popular for sledge-dog racing.

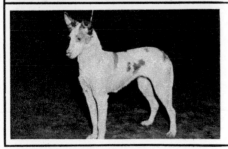

IBIZAN HOUND ■
The Ibizan Hound is a dog built for speed which differs from other Greyhound types in having large, upright ears. They are usually smooth coated and chestnut and white in colour.

IRISH SETTER ■ ● ▲

Like all the setters, the Irish Setter has a sentimental, dreamy expression. The glorious rich chestnut of the coat has led to more being kept as pets and showdogs than gundogs.

IRISH TERRIER ■ ● ▲

The Irish Terrier earned the nickname of the 'red devil' because the fieriness of its temper matched the red of its coat. They combine their cavalier attitude to the canine race with a remarkable love and loyalty towards their masters.

IRISH WATER SPANIEL ■ ● ▲

A coat of liver ringlets contrasting with a smooth face and tail give the Irish Water Spaniel a remarkable appearance. They are excellent water dogs with the endearing habit of playing the clown when off duty.

IRISH WOLFHOUND ■ ● ▲

The Irish Wolfhound accompanied the Celtic chieftains into battle and needed size and courage to pull down the enemy horsemen. After near extinction in the nineteenth century, they are now well established.

ITALIAN GREYHOUND ■ ● ▲

A dainty Greyhound in miniature, the Italian has a high-stepping gait all its own. They have been royal favourites in past centuries.

JAPANESE SPANIEL ■ ● ▲

These decorative toy spaniels most resemble the Pekinese, but are higher on the leg and carry a less profuse coat, which is always white with either black or red patches.

KARABASH (ANATOLIAN) DOG ■

These massive dogs come from Turkey where they are used to guard the flocks against wolves. The coat is medium-short, dense and fawn or brindle in colour. They stand about twenty-nine inches at the shoulder.

KEESHOND ■ ● ▲

The Keeshond has a dense, off-standing coat of grey, with delicate pencilling round the eyes and lighter shadings on the legs and tail. They have always been family watchdogs with little desire to roam.

KERRY BLUE TERRIER ■ ● ▲

Puppies of this breed are born black and acquire their blue coat when adult. They are unusual for a terrier in having soft, wavy coats which can be trimmed with scissors.

KING CHARLES SPANIEL ■ ● ▲

The Americans call the King Charles Spaniel the English Toy Spaniel. The breed was a favourite one with King Charles II. They are divided into four varieties according to colour: Black and Tan, Tricolour, Ruby and Blenheim.

KOMONDOR ●

The Komondor is a large, muscular dog used in the past to protect herds of cattle from wolves on the Hungarian plains. The coat must be white and is long, soft and woolly, felting into impenetrable mats.

KUVASZ ■ ●

The Kuvasz was once the guardian and companion of the Hungarian nobility. Now rather smaller than the giants of the past the dog should stand about twenty-six inches at the shoulder and have a soft, wavy, white coat.

LABRADOR RETRIEVER ■ ● ▲

The willing nature of the Labrador has led to its present popularity in all fields. The coat, though short, is dense and weather resisting and usually either black or yellow in colour.

LAKELAND TERRIER ■ ● ▲

The Lakeland Terrier is a smart, alert dog which often wins high awards in the show ring. Colours include black and tan, and red.

LHASA APSO ■ ● ▲

This watchful and hardy breed is the only Tibetan dog recognized by the American Kennel Club. The coat is harsh and long, and though golden shades are preferred any colour is permissible.

MALTESE TERRIER ■ ● ▲

The Maltese should be a vigorous little dog under that long, silky white coat. The dark eyes contribute to the charming expression.

Buttons X

MANCHESTER TERRIER ■ ● ▲

The sleek, wide-awake appearance of the Manchester Terrier is accentuated by the gleaming black coat with its rich tan markings. These dogs are game and vivacious as befits a breed used for ratting.

MAREMMA ■

The Maremma is an Italian sheepdog used for protecting the flocks. The coat is harsh, wavy and white but the dog is neither so big nor so well known as the Pyrenean Mountain Dog.

MASTIFF ■ ● ▲

Great size is important in the Mastiff, provided it is combined with a powerful, well-knit frame. Despite a horrific past, the modern dogs are reliable in temperament and dignified in appearance.

MEXICAN HAIRLESS ■

The Mexican Hairless Dog comes in two sizes, the larger of which is about the size and shape of a Manchester Terrier. Always great rarities, the skin colour can be bronze, elephant-grey or black.

MINIATURE PINSCHER ■ ● ▲

The 'Minpin' is a stylish little toy dog with erect ears and a short docked tail. As they are good watchdogs with a clean, neat appearance, their numbers are increasing on both sides of the Atlantic.

NEWFOUNDLAND ■ ● ▲

The Newfoundland is a handsome dog with a gentle, tractable disposition. The dull black coat is slightly oily and water-resistant as befits a dog which is a magnificent swimmer credited with saving a number of lives.

NORWEGIAN BUHUND ■

The Buhund is used as a watchdog and cattle dog in its native land. They are medium-sized, hardy dogs of the Spitz type. Most Buhunds in Britain are wheaten but black and red are also permissible.

NORWICH TERRIER ■ ● ▲

Usually red or wheaten in colour the straight wiry coat almost forms a mane over the shoulders. In America the ears can either be erect or drop. In Britain the drop-eared variety has been given separate breed status as the Norfolk Terrier.

OLD ENGLISH SHEEPDOG ■ ● ▲

The Bobtail was once a cattle dog but is now kept solely as a show dog and pet. Being a thick-set dog with a profuse, hard coat, the Old English Sheepdog looks clumsy but is in fact strong and agile.

OTTERHOUND ■ ●

The outer coat of the Otterhound should be crisp and oily and it is aided in the water by having webbed feet. In America a number of enthusiasts are devoted to the breed's welfare but in Britain they have seldom been shown and are low in numbers.

PAPILLON ■ ● ▲

The large, obliquely held ears of the Papillon resemble the wings of a butterfly, after which the breed is named. They have been favourites among European nobility since the sixteenth century. There is a rare, drop-eared variety known as Phalène.

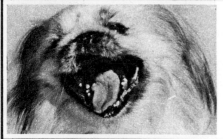

PEKINESE ■ ● ▲

The arrogant charm of the Pekinese has made it a favourite toy dog the world over. They are hardy, well-built dogs with heavy bone and independent personalities. The profuse coat should be rather coarse and all colours are permissible.

PEMBROKESHIRE WELSH CORGI ■ ● ▲
This is the more popular of the Welsh Corgis, possibly owing to royal patronage. The tail is docked short or is absent altogether and various shades of red are the commonest colour.

POINTER ■ ● ▲
The Pointer presents a lithe, muscular appearance, in keeping with a dog whose work was to range widely over moorland finding game. A minority still work as gundogs, particularly in America, where they are popular in Field Trial events.

POMERANIAN ■ ● ▲
The Pomeranian is really a miniature Spitz. At first glance the dog resembles nothing so much as an active, buoyant powder puff, with an intelligent, foxy face framed by a profuse mane and frill.

POODLE ■ ● ▲
The phenomenal success of the Poodle is due to many things, but not the least is the breed's cleverness. Three sizes are recognized separately and the coat can be any solid colour.

PUG ■ ● ▲
The square, cobby shape of the Pug gives a well upholstered look. Their origins are obscure but they probably came from the Far East like many of the short-faced toy breeds.

PULI ■ ●
The Puli is a medium-sized Hungarian sheepdog with a nimble, springy gait and a remarkable coat. The outer coat is long, soft and profuse and tangles with the undercoat to form cords. A weather-worn, dull black is the preferred colour.

PYRENEAN MOUNTAIN DOG ■ ● ▲
Called the Great Pyrenees in America, this large dog is predominately white in colour. As well as their majestic appearance, they are valued for their kindly, protective natures.

RHODESIAN RIDGEBACK ■ ● ▲

The Rhodesian Ridgeback combines courage with endurance. The distinguishing feature of the breed is the ridge of hair lying in the opposite direction to the rest of the coat and extending along the spine from the shoulders to the hip bones.

ROTTWEILER ■ ● ▲

When its original job as a cattle drover ended, the Rottweiler succeeded as a police and army dog. The glossy coat is black with tan markings.

ST. BERNARD ■ ● ▲

The romantic legends that surround the St. Bernard ensure that it is recognized everywhere. Only its enormous size prevents it from becoming more popular.

SALUKI ■ ● ▲

The Saluki is one of the most graceful and one of the fastest of dogs. The silky coat is smooth except for the feathering on the ears, legs and tail.

SAMOYED ■ ● ▲

The harsh, stand-off coat of the Samoyed is usually silvery-white. They were sledge and herd dogs from the tundras of Russia. The smiling expression is a breed feature.

SCHIPPERKE ■ ● ▲

The appearance of the Schipperke suggests a mischievous, little dog full of bounce and pep. They have been in existence a long while as watchdogs and barge dogs in the Netherlands.

SCHNAUZER ■ ● ▲

This German breed has the appearance of a terrier but more the character of a sheepdog. The Schauzer comes in three sizes, with a wiry coat which is either pepper and salt, or black.

SCOTTISH TERRIER ■ ● ▲
Among the endearing qualities of the Scottie are its staunchness and loyalty. The jet black coat is so universal that the brindle and wheaten colours are almost unknown.

SEALYHAM TERRIER ■ ● ▲
The Sealyham is a small dog with a great deal of power, substance and gameness. Most of its admirers though, fall for the roguish sense of humour.

SHETLAND SHEEPDOG ■ ● ▲
The sweetness of expression of the Shetland Sheepdog adds to the attractions of this Collie in miniature. Tricolours, sables and blue merles are the recognized colours.

SHIH TZU ■ ▲
The Shih Tzu is a very active, sound little dog of Tibetan origin. The long, dense coat gives a chrysanthemum effect.

SILKY TERRIER ■ ● ▲
A toy dog developed in Australia, the Sydney Silky has the forceful, friendly character of a terrier breed. The ears are erect and the soft, blue and tan coat is of moderate length.

SKYE TERRIER ■ ● ▲
Skye Terriers are an old breed which reached the height of its popularity in Victorian times. The body of a Skye should be long and low, and the hard, straight coat should be floor length.

SOFT-COATED WHEATEN TERRIER ■
Like the other Irish terriers, the Soft-coated Wheaten is a game vermin killer. The type has remained unchanged for a good many years and the soft, wavy coat needs no trimming.

STAFFORDSHIRE BULL TERRIER ■ ● ▲
Dogs like the Staffordshire Bull Terrier were used in the past for organized dog fighting. With such a past it is not suprising that this breed is both tenacious and brave. American dogs differ considerably from the British.

SUSSEX SPANIEL ■ ● ▲
A rolling gait when moving, and a coat of rich, golden liver, distinguish the Sussex Spaniel. They have never been popular as gundogs because they don't work silently, and they are rarely seen on the show bench.

TIBETAN SPANIEL ■ ▲
This little spaniel is gay and independent, loving towards its owners and aloof with strangers. They should be well balanced dogs without the enormous coat and flat face of the Pekinese.

TIBETAN TERRIER ■ ▲
This breed resembles an Old English Sheepdog in miniature. The Tibetan Terrier though, has a tail which is carried gaily. The profuse coat is long and fine and can be any colour except chocolate.

VISZLA ■ ● ▲
The Viszla or Hungarian Pointer is expected both to find game and retrieve it after it has been shot. This then is a multiple purpose gundog with a short coat of a rusty-gold colour.

WEIMARANER ■ ● ▲
The breed standard of the Weimaraner stresses that its hunting ability is of the greatest importance. These dogs are sometimes nicknamed 'ghost dogs' because of their amber eyes and silver-grey coat.

WELSH SPRINGER SPANIEL ■ ● ▲
The Welsh Springer has been a purebred working dog for many centuries. Slightly smaller than the English Springer, the Welsh has a dark red and white coat.

WELSH TERRIER ■ ● ▲
The Welsh is another sporting, black and tan terrier.

WEST HIGHLAND WHITE TERRIER ■ ● ▲
The West Highland White is a self confident, jaunty dog, related to the Cairn Terrier and sharing its hardy physique. The white coat, being harsh, picks up very little dirt.

WHIPPET ■ ● ▲
Whippet-racing is a popular sport as these pint-sized Grey-hounds have phenomenal powers of acceleration. These quiet, decorative dogs can have coats of any colour.

YORKSHIRE TERRIER ■ ● ▲
The show Yorkshire Terrier is a fancier's dog for the length and texture of the coat preclude the animal living a free life, For those willing to sacrifice perfection of coat, the Yorkshire Terrier makes an active and alert pet.

ACKNOWLEDGMENTS

BLACK AND WHITE

The picture on page 48 is reproduced by Gracious Permission of H. M. The Queen. Ashmolean Museum, Oxford 46, 47B; Australian News and Information Bureau 131C, 148E; Barnaby's Picture Library 34T, 39, 50C, 60T, 64, 65, 70, 71, 92, 102, 103T, 103B, 104, 105, 110, 119B, 129, 130A, 133D, 139B, 140A, 141A, 143B, E, 150B, C; B.B.C. 82BL, 86, 87, 88, 89, 90T; Bord Failte Eireann 14; British Museum 25, 27, 46T; Central Press Photos 41, 42, 63, 99T, 99B, 101T, 106BR, 121, 125, 138B, 141D, 144A, D, F, 147C, F; C.M. Cooke & Son 130B, C, 131A, B, F, G, 132A, G, 133A, B, C, D, 134A, C, D, E, 137A, B, C, D, 138A, D, E, F, 139A, C, D, E, 140B, C, D, 141B, C, E, F, 142A, B, D, E, F, 143A, C, 144B, E, G, 145A, B, C, E, 146B, C, 147B G, 148A, B, C, D, G, 149A, B, C, D, 150A; Denver Art Museum 22; Dorset Evening Echo 107T, 107B; Dulwich College Picture Gallery 49; Thomas Fall 146E; Fox Photos 126T, 127T; Giraudon 5, 11, 15, 24; Mrs Garrish, Rudgwick, Sussex 142G; Hamlyn Group Library 19; High Commissioner for New Zealand 29T, 29B, 34C, 40B; E.O. Hoppe 34B, 62; Imperial War Museum 93T, 93B; Mrs Keswick, Dumfries, Scotland 50L, 134F, 143D; Keystone Press Agency 66T, 68T, 72, 73, 80, 81, 109T, 111, 114BL; Mrs Lewin, Strood, Kent 144C; The Mansell Collection 7, 12, 20, 21, 61; The Collection of the Marchioness of Cholmondeley 54; His Grace the Duke of Marlborough: Photo A.M. Illingworth 44L; Metro Goldwyn Meyer 82T, 83, 91; R.G. Mowat, Glasgow 106TL; National-museum, Stockholm 59; Paramount Pictures 84, 90BR; P.D.S.A. 94, 100, 101B, 106TR, 120; Photo Researchers 32, 137F, 142C, 149E, 150A; Pictorial Parade, N.Y. 79; Pictorial Press Frontispiece, 13, 40T, 50R, 74, 112, 132B, 134B, 137E, 143F, 146A, D, 147A, E, 148C; Popperfoto 10, 82BR; Press Association 138C; Anne Roslin-Williams 144G; R.S.P.C.A. 108; Mrs R. Stenning, Pangbourne, Berks. 60B; Syndication International 8, 31, 33, 66, 67B, 69T, 106BL, 109B, 119T, 122, 123, 124, 126B, 127B, 128, 145D, 150D; W. Suschitzky 9; The Tate Gallery 51; Thames Television 85; Sally Anne Thompson 28, 114BR, 130A, 132C, D, 134F, 140E, 143E, 146F; John Topham 30, 43; United Artists 90BL; Roger Viollet 16; Trustees of the Wallace Collection 45, 52, 53; Lionel Young 68B, 69B.

COLOUR

Alpha 75; Barnaby's 96T, 135TL; B.B.C. 78T, 78B; F.P.G. 95, 117T, 117B; Keystone Press Agency 18, 36—37B, 115; Musee de la Ville de Strasbourg 55; Nationalmuseum, Stockholm 58; Photo Researchers 96B; Pictorial Press 76B; Sally Anne Thompson 17, 35, 36T, 37T, 38, 76T, 135TR, 135BL, 135BR, 136TL, 136BL, 136BR; Scala 56, 57; Syndication International 77, 97, 98, 118, 135BL, 136TR.